SCOTLAND IN O RAPHS

# ST ANDREWS

AYMOND LAMONT-BROWN

ALAN SUTTON PUBLISHING LIMITED

Alan Sutton Publishing Limited
Phoenix Mill • Far Thrupp • Stroud
Gloucestershire • GL5 2BU

First published 1996



**British Library Cataloguing in Publication Data**
A catalogue record for this book is available from the British Library.

ISBN 0–7509-1145-X

Typeset in 10/12 Perpetua.
Typesetting and origination by
Alan Sutton Publishing Limited.
Printed in Great Britain by
Ebenezer Baylis, Worcester.

## The St Andrews Preservation Trust Limited

The Trust was founded in 1937, the first such trust in Scotland, with its main aim to preserve the ancient buildings of St Andrews. Today, with all the modern pressures on development, it receives opinion, and comments to the local planning authority on hundreds of planning applications each year, and does everything it can to influence preservation of what is best in St Andrews. The Trust Museum at 12 North Street contains many items that reflect the social history of the town, a costume collection, historic scrapbooks, furniture and clocks, ornaments, china and pictures. It also stages special exhibitions by local artists and craftsmen.

# Contents

Around the time that the College of St Salvator's, North Street, St Andrews, was combined in 1747 with the College of St Leonard to become known as United College, townsfolk began to notice the distinctive weathering of a certain stone above the carved coat of arms on the south front of the college tower. A contemporary visitor, John Reid of Fogo, Berwickshire, noted that it was taking on human features. Soon a story was built up around it by the town worthies. Directly in front of the college gate, at a spot now marked with the monogram P.H. in the cobbled paving, the Lutheran preacher Patrick Hamilton was executed at the stake on 29 February 1528. The outline of the face in stone was deemed by the credulous and mischievous to be the psychic imprint of his martyred gaze. It has intrigued visitors, artists and photographers ever since.

ST ANDREW: HIS BURGH, HIS SEE, HIS NATION

A number of portrayals of the apostle and martyr St Andrew of Bethsaida in Galilee are sited around St Andrews. The most spectacular is perhaps the depiction on the ceiling of the Council Chamber of the Town Hall. Above the lower stairs of the Council Chamber entrance is this wooden escutcheon showing the apostle with the traditional *crux decusata* of his martyrdom and the wild boar and oak tree of the burgh's coat of arms. Possibly of the sixteenth century (but bearing the curious date 1115), the escutcheon comes from Holy Trinity Church and was probably placed on the end of the pew occupied by the Provost and Town Council. St Andrews was formed by Bishop Robert some time between 1140 and 1150 out of the gift of the extant 'vil' of King David I. Bishop Robert also changed the name of the place from Kinrimund to St Andrews to honour the site of the shrine containing the apostle's relics within the then new cathedral. A medieval story tells how bones of St Andrew were brought from Patras by the Greek monk Regulus, and were set in a reliquary in what is now St Andrews to become the focal point of the saint's cult. On 13 August 1472, Pope Sixtus IV elevated the bishopric of St Andrews into an archbishopric and the burgh assumed the dignity of becoming the ecclesiastical capital of Scotland, whose inhabitants had chosen Andrew as their patron saint by 1286. On 28 February 1620 King James VI & I granted and confirmed by new charter the ancient documents making St Andrews a Royal Burgh.

# INTRODUCTION

Old photographs of St Andrews exert a strange power. In a single image decades of time are stripped away to reunite the modern viewer with his or her ancestors and roots. When the first crude photographs were captured in 1826 by such as the young Sardinian army officer Nicéphore Niépce, Queen Victoria was a German-speaking seven-year-old. Yet it was in Victorian St Andrews that the seeds of early photography were to be nurtured to put the burgh in the foreground of the history of photography.

In a way early Victorian St Andrews was an unexpected player in the history of the photographic image. At that time the burgh was in decline intellectually, socially and commercially, yet it contained residents of vision. One such was Sir David Brewster (1781–1868), Principal of the United College, who was to strike up a mutual interest in the new thoughts on photography with a young local doctor John Adamson (1809–70). Brewster and Adamson were leading lights in the foundation in 1838 of the St Andrews Literary and Philosophical Society; thus photography was to be an important documentary tool in setting up the records of the science museum at United College. Dr Adamson's experiments encouraged and influenced his younger brother Robert (1821–48) to set up a calotype studio on Calton Hill, Edinburgh, in 1843. The portraits taken by Robert Adamson and his partner David Octavius Hill (1802–70) have hardly been equalled. Adamson also encouraged Thomas Rodger (1833–83) to become a professional calotypist; he set up the first photographic studio in St Andrews at his home at 6 St Mary's Place.

The period of history represented in this collection shows St Andrews when it was a much smaller place, before the burgeoning of the burgh to the south and west.

Today St Andrews is still a haven for scholars, sportsmen and seniors seeking the character richness of the burgh for their retirement. All this, of course, is nothing new. Scholars have been associated with the town since the university was given a charter of privileges by the diocesan Bishop Henry Wardlaw in 1411; golf was played in St Andrews before 1457, for that was the year King James II signed an 'Act Forbidding Golf'; and in the latter years of the nineteenth century retired imperial administrators flocked to St Andrews to spend their declining days in some splendour. And tourism is nothing new either, for St Andrews of the Middle Ages was firmly on Europe's pilgrim routes because of the fame of the shrine of the apostle within its cathedral.

Down the centuries St Andrews has absorbed, inaugurated and answered change. Old pictures show just how much has altered, but within these pages a spirit of old St Andrews remains reflected in all that is new.

*Section One*

# Early Exposures

*An original portrait from his St Mary's Place studio of Thomas Rodger and his daughter Jenny, 1860s. A pioneer St Andrews photographer, Thomas Rodger (1833–83) contributed greatly to the early history of photography in Scotland. He was a laboratory and photographic assistant to Dr John Adamson, and he learned the daguerreotype system of photography before taking up a course of medical studies in the late 1840s. Dr Adamson urged Rodger to establish a studio in St Andrews from where he was to produce prints for prestigious exhibitions and competitions. His studio was closed in the early 1900s and much of his work was destroyed.*

Hope Park Church at the junction of Market Street and Howard Place, photographed by Thomas Rodger soon after its opening on 23 November 1865. The foundations of a manse were laid in 1866 next door in Howard Place. The unmade road marks the western extremities of Market Street with the unfinished houses of St Mary's Place (left) and Lockhart Place (right).

At the eastern end of Market Street stood the burgh's Old Town Hall or Tolbooth, seen here in Dr John Adamson's picture of about 1860. It is likely that there were four municipal town houses on this site, the first dating from very soon after the burgh had been founded by Bishop Robert, *c.* 1140. The building developed as a two storey edifice with outside stair (removed 1818), police cell, debtors' prison and 'thief's hole'. On the eastern elevation can be seen the butter market and hustings for political meetings. This was demolished in 1862.

Thomas Rodger's plate of about 1865 showing South Street looking east. On the left is the south transept of Holy Trinity Church as rebuilt 1798–99. The new Town Hall stands at the junction with Queen's Gardens, which had opened as Queen's Street in 1858.

Dr John Adamson (1809–70) as photographed by his protégé Thomas Rodger, *c.* 1865. Adamson was Medical Officer for St Andrews by 1848, the year the town was hit by cholera. He was responsible for the founding of the town's Cottage Hospital and was in the forefront of modernising the town. Adamson lived at 127 South Street, where the present post office stands, and just off the foreground of the picture above.

Walter Fenton, pilot, *c.* 1860. He lost his leg at the Battle of Trafalgar, 21 October 1805. He used to pilot ocean-going vessels up the River Eden to Haig's Distillery at Guardbridge.

A distinguished St Andrean who lived at 173 South Street was David Hay Fleming (1849–1931). He devoted much of his life to the study of Scottish and St Andrews history and wrote several guides to the burgh. The son of a South Street china merchant, Fleming served on the Town Council from 1881 to 1884.

South Street, looking towards the West Port: note the pedestal flower urns. Lime trees were planted in 1879–80. On the right are the Albert Buildings at Logies Lane, designed by William Scott in 1844; beyond is the site of the Royal Hotel (1844–57), Dr Adamson's house at no. 127, and Professor of Moral Philosophy Dr Thomas Chalmer's (1780–1847) home at no. 129.

William 'Buff' Trail poses in a St Andrews carter's yard in about 1865. Trail was nicknamed 'Silly Wullie' because of his mental deficiency and made a living delivering packages, running (sometimes wild goose) errands and selling papers in the town.

Thomas Rodger's 1864 print of Blackfriar's Chapel, showing the ruined sixteenth-century north transept of the monastery of the Dominican Friars, said to have been founded by Bishop William Wishart of St Andrews in 1274. The chapel fronts architect William Burn's Madras College founded in 1832 by Dr Andrew Bell; it opened on 1 October 1833 and had been extended the year before Rodger took this photograph.

Dr Andrew Bell (1753–1832), taken from a *carte de visite* by Thomas Buist, *c.* 1860. Bell died the year before his college was opened. His epitaph in Westminster Abbey reads: 'The Author of the Madras System of Education', an allusion to his teaching work in India.

J. Valentine's picture of Priory House (demolished 1957) and South Street, *c.* 1878. On the left can be seen College Hall (1868; then Bishophall). This complex was taken over by St Leonards girls' school (founded 1877) in 1882. Priory House was set on the foundations of the Subprior's house (*c.* 1143) of the Augustinian Priory that abutted the cathedral. At this date the foundations of the priory refectory (left forefront) had not been excavated and rebuilt by the Marquis of Bute.

Sir Hugh Lyon Playfair (1786–1861) being pushed in a sedan-chair mounted on a later chassis, *c.* 1855. Provost of St Andrews from 1842 to 1861, he is credited with 'rebuilding' the burgh. His home was in the former priory precinct at St Leonards, where he established a noteworthy garden which he opened to the public. As Honorary Curator of Crown properties in St Andrews he oversaw the renovation and cleaning out of the castle policies, and supervised the long overdue tidying of the cathedral ruins.

The ruined nave and surviving west gable of St Andrews cathedral, *c.* 1878. On the right is situated the Fisher School (1856) which became the East Infants' School. North Street widens into Gregory's Green and sixteenth-century Deans Court fronts the cathedral entrance.

John-Patrick Crichton-Stuart, 3rd Marquis of Bute (1847–1900), was elected Rector of the University of St Andrews in 1892 and became a benefactor of both town and gown. Bute was a keen restorer of ancient monuments and his fervent interest in ecclesiastical properties developed after his conversion to Catholicism – which provided Benjamin Disraeli (1804–81) with background for his novel *Lothair* (1870). Although the Barons of the Exchequer took possession of St Andrews cathedral ruins in 1826, the abutting priory fell to the ownership of Bute, and in 1946 it was given to the state by Major M.D.D. Crichton-Stuart.

Thomas Rodger's photograph, *c.* 1870, of the south elevation of The Pends. Built in about 1350, The Pends – *Pendentes*, an arched passage with chambers above – was the main gateway into the medieval priory precincts. A central supporting arch of the chambers had been removed in 1837–38.

St Andrews castle from the east, *c.* 1890. A bathing hut (with drying costumes) abuts the base of the castle's Great Hall which fell into the sea in 1801. A bathing pool was constructed here in 1904 where local fishermen had once beached their boats. Behind the medieval castle is Castlecliff House (*c.* 1877) with Castlegate House (1879) on the extreme left.

*SECTION TWO*

# MEANS OF GETTING AROUND

*A two-in-hand, four-wheeled brougham, with liveried coachman sits outside the Paterson family home at 16 Greyfriars Garden (founded as North Bell Street in 1834),* c. *1890. The carriage type was introduced to fashionable society by Henry Peter Brougham, 1st Baron Brougham and Vaux (1778–1868), the Scottish jurist, who became Lord Chancellor in Lord Melbourne's First Cabinet of 1834. Broughams came in various sorts and sizes – this being a double with lowering windows. One like this would have cost about 150 guineas in 1890.*

A sergeant of the Lowland Cycle Battalion poses with his BSA folding bicycle during the early days of the First World War (1914–18). Based at Cupar, the cyclists were common enough figures in and around St Andrews. The cycle battalions were units of the Territorial Army and grew out of the reorganisation of the military forces in 1908.

The Wilson family take a drive, *c.* 1906. James Wilson is driving and his father William sits beside him as they pass the West Lodge of Mount Melville Estate. The Wilsons had a garage and motor works at 193 South Street, as well as Alexandra Place. By 1903 the Motor Car Act had licensed vehicles and drivers and by 1906 there were 23,192 private cars in use in the UK.

Driver and passenger wait outside the Greyfriars Hotel in Greyfriars Garden. This was a temperance hotel descibed as 'family and commercial', and boasting the 'electric light'. The car is an Austin 12 of 1923–24 vintage; the 12 continued to be produced until 1934.

A butcher's delivery cart and driver wait patiently for orders outside Johnston's Livery Stables in Market Street. Most St Andrews shops sported a delivery cart as a version of the popular dog or market cart. In the 1890s they retailed at 25 to 60 guineas.

A pair of horses and grooms pose at St Nicholas Farm ready for an appearance at the annual St Andrews Horse Fair. The first Horse Parade took place on 19 September 1912 and was organised by Bailie Major Charles H. Morris of Dyer's Brae. Farmers, carter firms, contractors and commercial companies all exhibited well-groomed horses. The stated object of the parade was to 'encourage those in charge of horses to take an interest in the animals' comfort and to treat them kindly'. Prizes were awarded at a ceremony opposite the Central Bar, Market Street; this was followed by a gymkhana in Cockshaugh Park.

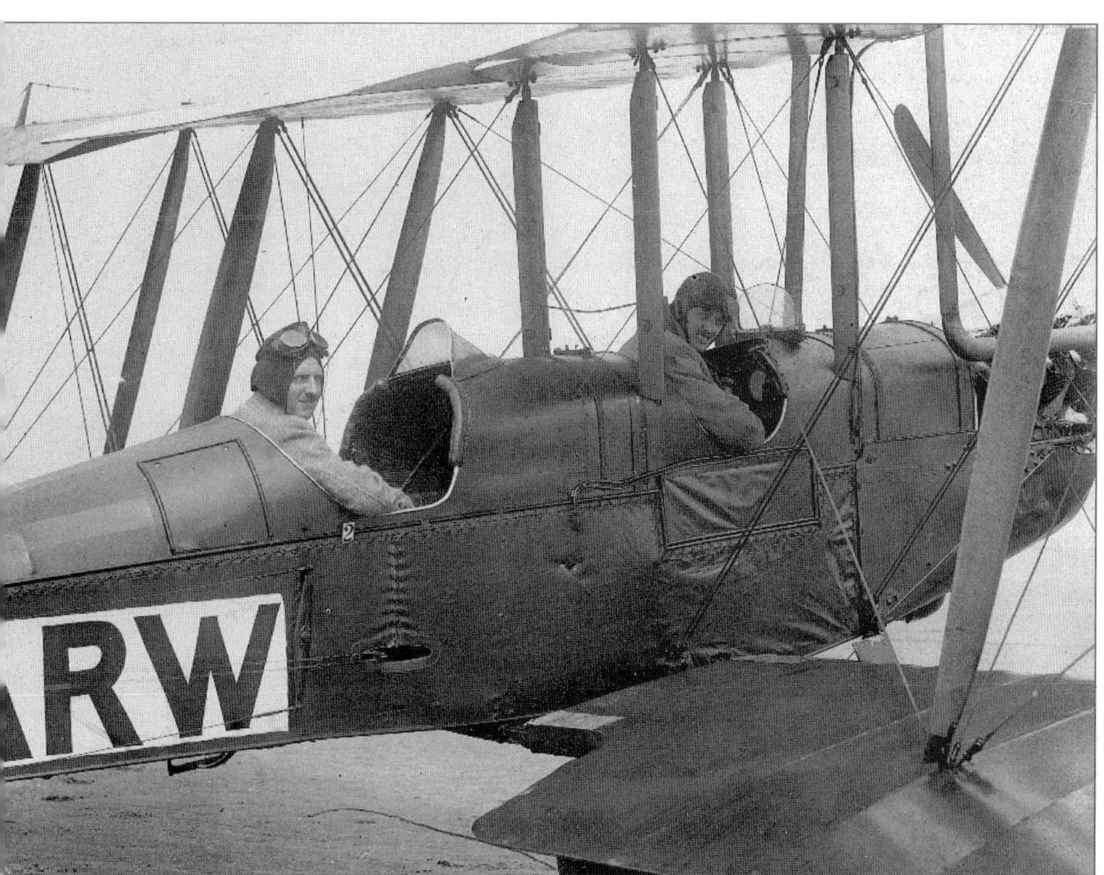


From time to time private plane pilots brought their craft to the West Sands for the entertainment of paying passengers to enjoy 'a flip' above the burgh. The passenger on this occasion in 1919 is thought to be Alfred George Scott (1892–1975). An architect in the town, he was a partner in the firm of Gillespie & Scott, Queens Gardens and was a founder of New Park School. He was Chairman of the New Picture House Board of Directors from 1932 to 1974, and a keen amateur actor. The aircraft is a Royal Aircraft Factory BE2e with the civilian registration G–EARW. Its former military serial number was C6963 and it was withdrawn from the civil register in 1921. Private planes of wealthy golfers used to land on the sands and there were regular barn-storming displays and 'flying circuses'.

William Johnston founded the livery stables which grew into Johnston's Garage (now the Mercat Wynd site). When Johnston died in 1917 the business was taken over by D.W. Methven at the 117 Market Street premises and at 104–8 North Street. The picture shows D.W. Methven (left, with riding breeches and bowler hat) standing by the door of the booking office where taxis (William Johnston had introduced the first taxis to St Andrews in 1906), cars and charabancs could be hired. On the right of the 1920s West Riding of Yorkshire-registered Austin taxi stands the driver Seath Martin, the mechanic James Smart and the garage manager Mr Miller.

J.M. Gray's Bedford 1932–33, Manchester-registered lorry and workmen at 41 North Street. The Younger Graduation Hall (1925–27) stands far left. The old fisher houses were to give way to the rectory for All Saints' Episcopal Church of 1938 and Gannochy House student residence of 1971.

*SECTION THREE*

# A HANDFUL OF CHARACTERS

*Operating from a recruiting office in Cupar and St Andrews, Corporal John Ripley VC stops to chat to prospective recruits at the West Port. Retired from the army as a Colour Sergeant since 1912, Ripley enlisted at the outbreak of the First World War as a Recruiting Sergeant in the 1st Battalion Black Watch. The only St Andrews man to win a VC, Ripley was a self-employed slater, chimney sweep and window cleaner; he died from injuries sustained by falling off a ladder at Castlecliff in 1933. He won his VC in 1915 for bravery at Rue de Bois, Battle of Aubers Ridge, Neuve Chapelle, France.*

Donald 'Donal' Blue (James McDougal, or Mitchell, 1846–1909) was raised by Mrs Watters of Baker Lane. He received his nickname from the blue jacket she dressed him in. At the end of his working life, as a ship's cook and a labourer, he worked at the Links as a caddie, sometimes giving golf tuition. The picture was taken at his own request in about 1903; he had it made into postcards to give to 'prospective clients' for his caddying services.

George Butters (b. 1822), photographed in 1901. A baker by trade, Butters was appointed Castle Keeper in 1892 by the then owners of the ruined castle, the St Andrews Town Council. From 1728 to 1808 the interior of the ruins was rented out for various purposes; in 1810 the first council 'keeper' was employed and the castle was excavated and made safe during the period 1857–1903. In 1911 the castle was taken into state ownership as an ancient monument.

'Caum' Eppie from the portrait by Thomas Rodger, 1860. One of St Andrews' Victorian characters, 'Caum' Eppie received her nickname from the old Scots word for a slate pencil; people used to whiten their hearths, windowsills and doorsteps with 'Caumstane'. Eppie sold this commodity from her basket around the doors. She always carried with her a large key; whenever anyone asked what it was the key of, Eppie would reply 'It's the key to Hell'.

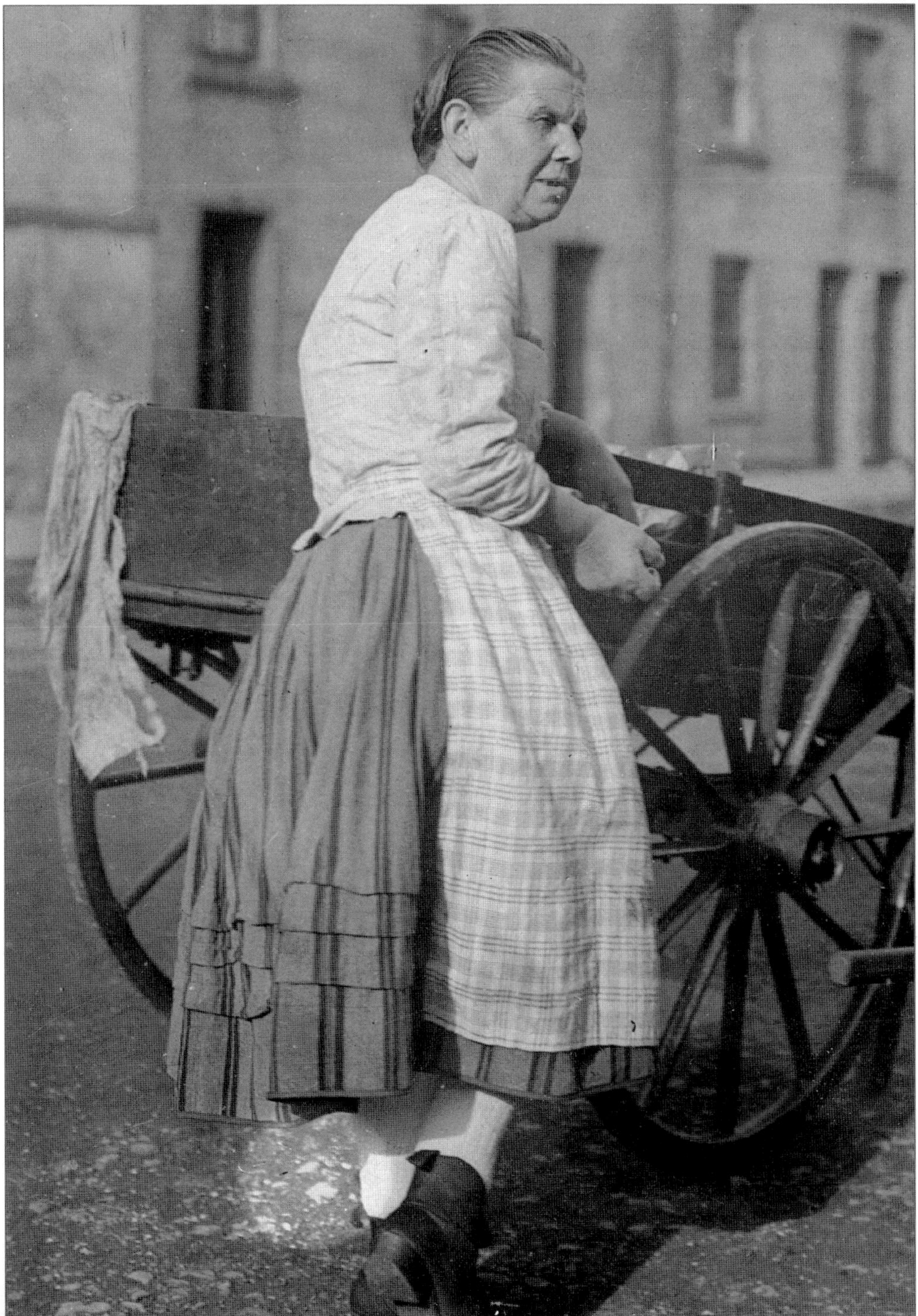

Mrs Henry Clark (1852–1927) – known locally only as 'Joan' – wore the distinctive costume of the traditional Scots fishwife: white stockings, elastic-sided boots, striped skirt over a multitude of coloured petticoats, and fisher apron. She sold flounders, white fish and cod from her barrow – here she is in North Street opposite the Younger Hall. She lived at 11 South Castle Street.

One of the many Victorian street vendors and itinerant jobbers, Pat Riley was photographed outside the West Door of Holy Trinity Church in about 1890. The railings have now long gone. Riley ground and sharpened household blades.

*SECTION FOUR*

# THE FISHERFOLK

*Peter Waters sits in the foreground baiting his lines at the east end of North Street. The houses, now demolished, gave way to the university's Younger Graduation Hall (1925–29), the residence of Gannochy House (1971) and All Saints' Rectory (1938). In medieval times this is where the Fisher Cross stood (it was removed around 1800) to denote the importance of the fisher quarter of the town, the home of a hard-working, colourful and independently minded community. This part of the quarter was known as the Ladyhead: a number of theories have been put forward for the name 'Ladyhead' – it may have been the name of rocks in the sea approach by the long pier; or from a ship's figurehead displayed here; or a stone madonna from the cathedral ruins, or Fisher Cross, built into the wall of the house opposite the Old Castle Tavern.*

James Hill Gourlay mends his nets while his son Alex rubs his eye. They are outside 33–35 North Street, now The Ladyhead Bookshop. The mercury barometer set in the wall was refurbished in 1988. Called 'Vice-Admiral Fitzroy's Storm Tubes' (Robert Fitzroy, 1805–65, was the first director of the Meteorological Department of the Board of Trade), they gave fishermen advance warning of worsening weather.

Children of the East Infants School, Gregory Place, pose with their teacher, *c.* 1885. It had been the Fishers' School of 1856 and is now sheltered housing in an area known as Kirkhill.

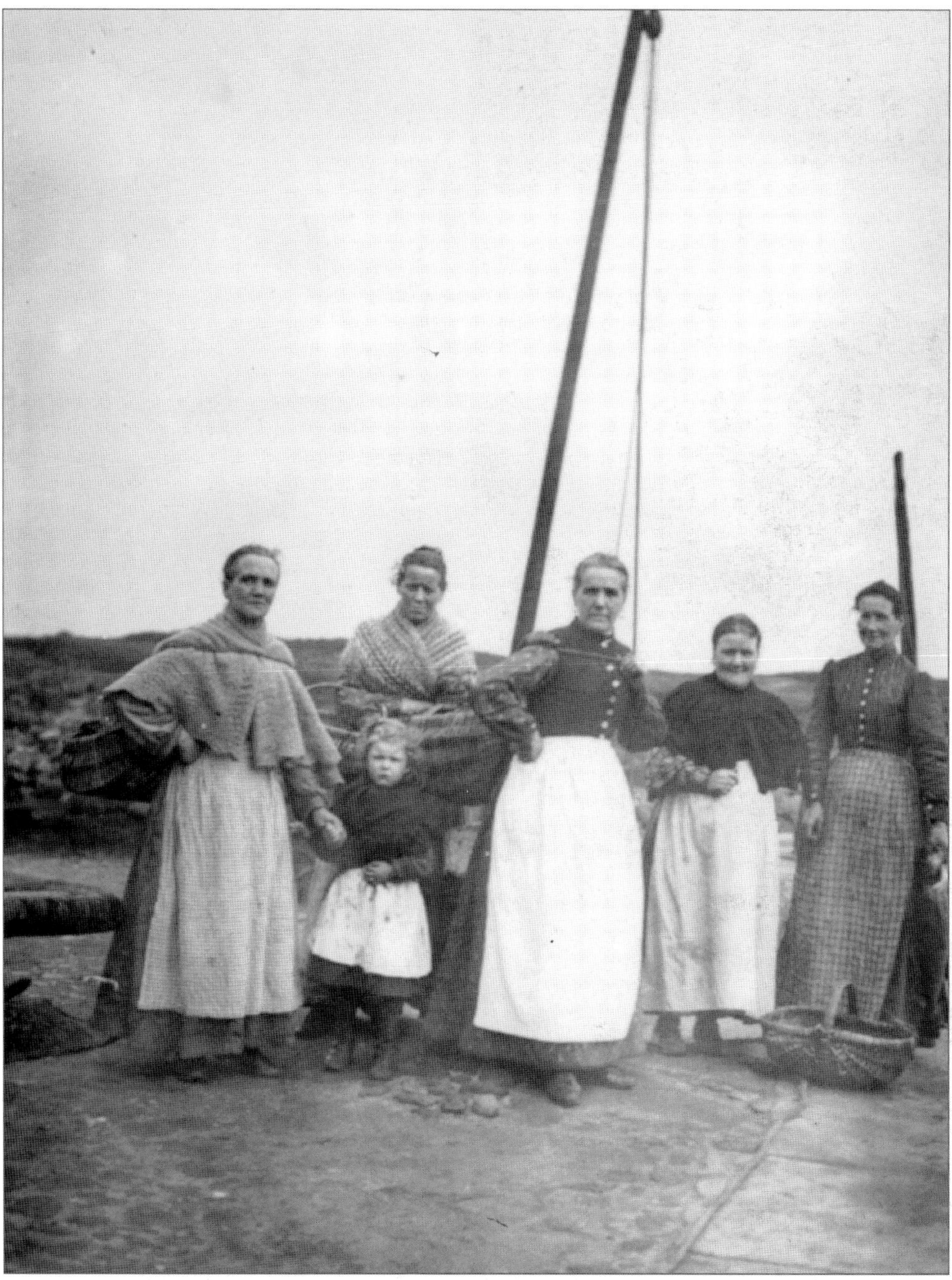

A group of fisherwomen assemble with their creels by St Andrews Harbour looking towards the East Bents, around the end of the First World War. They are dressed in traditional fisherfolk costume. Because of the hard life encountered by the fisherfolk many of them look prematurely aged. They have been identified as, left to right: Mary Duff (Mrs Hailey) with grand-daughter; Annie Hopkin (Mrs James Lister); Grace Duff (Mrs Bond); Teenie Bell (Mrs Hutchinson); and Bess Waters (Mrs Fowles). Because of similar surnames, individual eccentricities, or job varieties many St Andrews fisherfolk had nicknames. Teenie Bell had a footballer son with the childhood nickname of 'Tee Ta Toe'. As a small boy he had been sent to the baker's for three half-loaves; these he had asked for as 'tee ta toe'.

The rear of the tenements at The Shorehead, St Andrews Harbour, with the outside lavatories set in 'towers'. Many of the town's working people lived in overcrowded tenements like these which were named after ships of the line, for example the *Great Eastern*, *Great Western*, and the *Pembroke*; this one was called the *Royal George*. The site had been two taverns, a malthouse and fishermen's stores. By 1935 the flats were condemned and the site was rebuilt in 1965–66 as houses and flats.

Studio portrait of the St Andrews lifeboat crew of 1890 at a lifeboat demonstration. They have been identified thus: back row, from the left: R.Wilson, R. Duncan, W. Duncan, J. Gourlay, A. Gourlay. Second row: Andrew Gordon, William Chisholm, James Chisholm (Coxwain). Third row: Mr Miller, Lifeboat Officer, Mr Martin, Secretary of the Scottish Lifeboat Institute, J. Chisholm, Dave Melville. Front row: the brothers Thomas and Joseph Hutchinson. The first lifeboat for St Andrews was acquired in about 1800 as a consequence of the wrecking of the sloop *Janet* out of Macduff, Banffshire. A boat house for rescue vessels was erected at the East Bents in 1803. The burgh was to retain its own lifeboat until 1938. By 1890 the crew worked out of a main lifeboat station at Boarhills aboard the *John and James Mills* (1881).

The schooner *Nelly* at St Andrews Harbour – by the tenement *Royal George* – loading with potatoes for various ports, *c.* 1910. She also carried coal from the Tyne ports. On her return to St Andrews she often brought up to 200 tons of salt per voyage for Wilson's Ironmongers, South Street.

The *Catherine Black* (DE175) lies at The Shore by the Mill Port, St Andrews Harbour, *c.* 1910. Those aboard have been identified thus, left to right: Stewart Fenton; Alex Gourlay, Willie Gourlay, John Waters, -?-, Bobbie Duncan, David Waters, Jamie Gourlay, Geordie Brown, Jamie Litster, ? Cunningham, -?-, Sandy Kirk, Jonnie Himmerman, Bill Cross.

The lifeboat crew of the *John and Sarah Hatfield*. This was the last of St Andrews' own lifeboats and was a 25 ft, self-righting Rubie Class Type vessel put into commission on 12 May 1910, around the time this photograph was taken. She served until 1938 when the vessel was sold to Valvona of Portobello as a pleasure cruiser. From left to right, the crewmen are: Bob Duncan, Bob Cunningham, -?-, A. Hill Gourlay, David Fenton, A. Gordon, Jimmy Chisholm.

The lifeboat crew pose at the rear entry of their base at the sea foot of Woodburn Place. Coxwain Chisholm is in the centre with seaman's cap.

The wreck of the barque *Prinses Wilhelmina* lies at the West Sands, St Andrews, near to the rocks by the Bruce Embankment. Two of her three masts are still in place and a portion of rigging. The process of salvage is under way. A storm had broken out in St Andrews Bay on 29 September 1912 and raged for several days. On 1 October it had increased in severity and one of the casualties was the *Prinses Wilhelmina* from the medieval port of Halmstad on the Kattegat coast, Sweden. At first she was embayed and was driven on to the rocks near St Andrews castle where nine seamen were rescued by the local lifeboatmen. Deprived of her main mast the barque disengaged herself and drifted through the breakers to settle at the West Sands. Her cargo of timber for Longland & McAimish, Dundee, was mostly salvaged.

The wreck of the *Prinses Wilhelmina* was a source of public interest for some time. Here a group of Sunday strollers inspect the wreckage after church. Two girls from St Leonards School join the group at the right (their style of boaters – straw hats – with house colours had been introduced in 1909).

W. Patrick's emotive photograph of the St Andrews lifeboat the *John and Sarah Hatfield* returning to St Andrews Harbour after answering the distress flares of the sparling fishing smack *Resolute*, which had been caught in the storm of 29 September 1912. The 290 yard long pier had been given a concrete extension in 1898; there had been a lighthouse at the sea end until 1849.

J. Valentine's panoramic view of St Andrews Harbour area from the East Bents, *c.* 1878. Behind the line of the East Bents (which had had a concrete protecting wall erected in 1877) is the Inner Harbour set out in 1785–89. In the centre is the old Mill Port, with the seventeenth-century reconstructed Shore Mill to the right, and behind is the Old Abbey Mill and Brewhouse (disused since 1861) which was to be the site of the Sanatorium (1899) for St Leonards School. The Eastern cemetery by Pends Road is empty at this date (it was set out late in 1878). The Gas Works of 1835 is seen flanking Prior Hepburn's Walls, leading the eye right up behind the *Royal George* tenements at The Shorehead. The harbour walls were rebuilt in 1654 using stones from the ruined castle, and the quay was rebuilt and the harbour widened and deepened in 1845–46. The Cross Pier dates from 1722. The original long wooden pier at St Andrews was demolished by a storm in 1655 and a half-length pier was erected in 1656 from castle stone. A packet-boat sailed regularly from St Andrews to Leith from 1830 to 1914.

*SECTION FIVE*

# THE MONSTROUS GAME

*'In one hundred years time, this monstrous game will have taken over St Andrews.' (George John Whyte-Melville (1821–76), Scottish novelist and field sports authority, of Mount Melville, St Andrews, in conversation.) The picture shows the first and eighteenth holes of the Old Course, at the 1957 Open Championship; the Royal and Ancient Clubhouse (1854) is on the right. Arthur D'Arcy 'Bobby' Locke (South Africa) putts for the Championship. Golf has been played at St Andrews since at least 1457, the year King James II passed the first Act forbidding the playing of golf as it kept young men from their archery practice (thereby affecting state security) and their Sabbath devotions. In 1552 the first St Andrews Links Charter was signed by John Hamilton, Archbishop of St Andrews, guaranteeing the burgesses full ownership of the Links and the right to play golf thereon. The first golf tournament was held on the Old Course in 1857, and The Open Golf Championship (The Trophy) was instituted in 1872.*

HRH Prince Leopold (1853–84), Duke of Albany, eighth child and fifth son of Queen Victoria, became Captain of the Royal and Ancient Golf Club on 27 September 1876. The wilful, haemophiliac prince was photographed here by Thomas Rodger in 1865. On becoming Captain he was hosted by John Whyte-Melville of Mount Melville, and Thomas Rodger presented the prince with an album of photographs during the royal tour of the town.

In 1754 the Society of St Andrews Golfers was instituted to play over the Links annually for a silver club; the winner of the match was to become 'Captain of the Golf'. In 1834 King William IV agreed to become the Club's patron and thereafter the Club was styled 'Royal and Ancient'. At first they met here at the Union Parlour (now the site of Hamilton Hall students' residence), before the Royal and Ancient Clubhouse opened in 1854. The picture, dating from 1848, is arguably the first in golfing history portraiture.

Players and spectators gather at the eighteenth green on the Old Course for the finish of the first Open Tournament of 1857. Robert Chambers is seen here putting, and kneeling, to the left, is Sir Hugh Lyon Playfair (1786–1861), Provost of St Andrews from 1842 until his death, who was Captain of the Royal and Ancient in 1856. Martyrs' Monument (1842) is seen on the slope of The Scores; originally the Old Course started from beyond the knoll behind the cannon. Note the roughness of the green.

Thomas Rodger's photograph of *c.* 1855 showing 'Old Professionals' at the Links, looking towards the West Sands. From left to right are: James Wilson, -?-; Willie Dunn, Bob Andrews, Willie Park, Tom Morris Sr, Allan Robertson, D. Anderson and Bob Kirk. Many of the clubs they are using would be deemed illegal today.

J. Valentine's photograph, *c.* 1885, of players at the first and eighteenth of the Old Course, beside the Royal and Ancient Clubhouse, which lacks its upper balcony and second storey. Martyrs' Monument stands on the grassy knoll at The Scores with the early Catholic church – the 'Tin Tabernacle' of 1884 – beyond. The caddies' shelter by the eighteenth has not yet been built, but the flagstaff from the Dumbarton-built tea clipper *Cutty Sark* (launched 1869) is in place. Nor has the Grand Hotel (1895) appeared at the right-hand side of The Scores and Golf Place.

'It is delightful to see a whole town given up to golf; to see the butcher and the baker and the candlestick maker shouldering his clubs as soon as his day's work is done and making a dash for the Links.' Thus wrote Bernard Darwin, the golf course historian, in 1910. This photograph, dated *c.* 1850, shows in the left group (in light suits) Tom Morris Sr, Robert Cathcart of Pitcairlie, and D. Anderson; and right of the small boy (Jamie Anderson who went on to win three successive Open Championships) are Alan Robertson, Wallace of Balgrummo, and Hay Wemyss. At this time golf was free to all. In 1912 green fees were introduced, but it was not until 1946 that St Andrews ratepayers were required to pay to play.

A ladies' golf match, *c.* 1890. The first woman golfer at St Andrews is said to have been Mary, Queen of Scots in 1567, but it took 300 years for the first Ladies' Putting Club to be instituted. This was to be the first women's golf club in Scotland, and the St Rules' Ladies' Club (clubhouse Gibson Place) was founded in 1898, while the St Regulus Ladies' Golf Club was founded before the First World War, with a permanent clubhouse at Pilmour Place in 1949.

Autograph hunters in the flowing fashions of the day gather to the north of Scholar's Bunker on the Old Course, some time after 1890. The Links had been purchased by George Cheape of Strathtyrum in 1848, and they were bought back for the town in 1893; they were to remain 'public property' via the Parliamentary Act of 1894.

Tom Morris Sr (1821–1908) seen here at the starter's box of the Old Course, was born in North Street, the son of a letter carrier; he started to play golf when he was a small child. He attended Madras College, was apprenticed to Alan Robertson as a golf-club maker and continued his trade after his move to Prestwick. Morris was Open Golf Champion in 1861, 1862, 1864 and 1866. In 1864 he was appointed Professional Golfer and Green-Keeper to the Royal and Ancient Golf Club at £50 a year; he held the position until 1903. The 354 yard, par 4, 18th green of the Old Course is named in his honour.

Tom Morris Sr's funeral cortège makes its way down cobbled South Street towards the cathedral cemetery. It passes the end of Church Street where the parish church of Holy Trinity is being rebuilt, 1907–9. At the opposite corner (where Innes's Bookshop is now) stood the Type Foundry of 1742–44 and the birthplace of Andrew Bell (1753–1832), founder of the Madras College.

Mrs P.G. Tait speaks to Andrew Kirkcaldy at the 17th green, the Road Hole, *c.* 1910. A colourful character, Andrew Kirkcaldy was Professional to the Royal and Ancient Golf Club from 1910 to 1934. Mrs Tait – mother of amateur champion Frederick 'Freddie' Guthrie Tait – was the wife of Professor P.G. Tait, the mathematician and philosopher.

Here Joe Kirkwood is bunkered at the Strath bunker (the 172 yard High Hole) on the 11th during the 1921 Open Championship, won that year by Jock Hutchinson of the USA. The Open Championship was held at St Andrews from 1873 and the Amateur Championship from 1886.

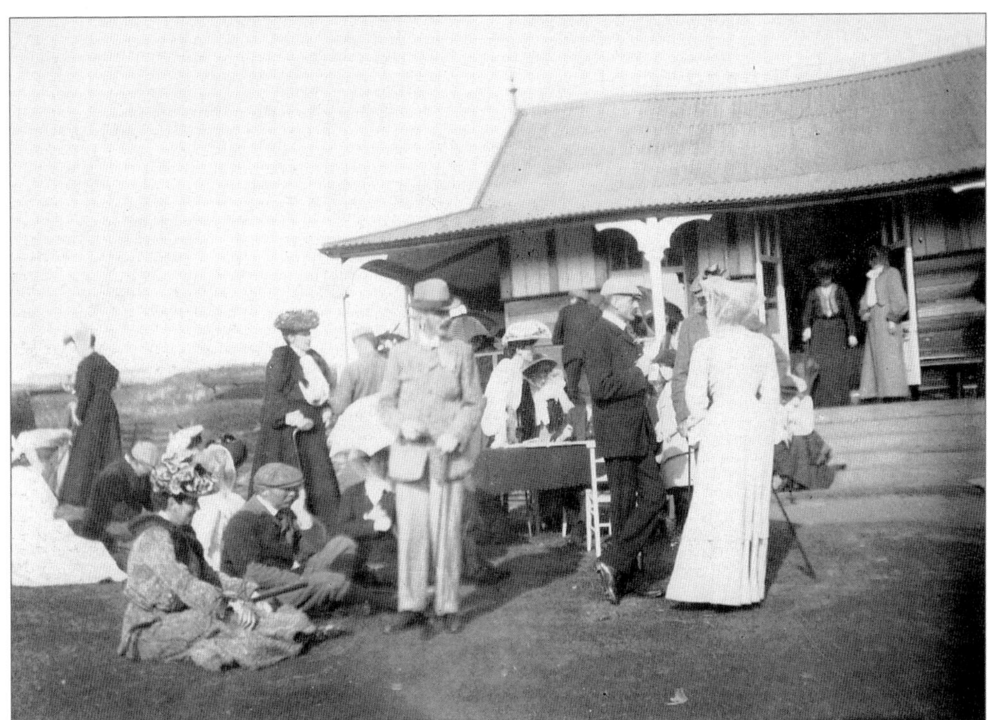

A crowd gathered for a competition at the Clubhouse (*c.* 1870) of the Ladies' Putting Green, known in local parlance as 'The Himalayas', *c.* 1910. Interest in golf among women was given a boost in 1906 when Miss Thompson became Ladies' Golf Champion.

W. Patrick's photograph – made into a popular postcard – of Miss Maud Titterton teeing off at the 1st Hole, in front of the Royal and Ancient Clubhouse in 1908. This was in the Ladies' Amateur Championship which she won.

Prominent Scottish professional champion Laurance Buddo Ayton tees up at the 461 yard Road Hole, the 17th. In the background is a well-known hazard, the Swilken Bridge, over the Swilken Burn. The bridge marks the old way across the Links to the burgh's ancient harbour in the Eden Estuary and the mussel beds.

Arthur Stanley Butler, Professor of Natural Philosophy, enjoys a round of golf with Andrew Lang (1844–1912), watched by an unknown caddie. The first canvas golf club container appeared in 1890. Lang was educated at Edinburgh Academy and matriculated at St Andrews University in 1861 and at Oxford in 1868. He became a popular journalist, poet and essayist and was conferred D.Laws *honoris causa* at St Andrews in 1885. In 1888 he was first Gifford Lecturer within the university. Lang spent most of the winter months in St Andrews, and in 1893 published his idiosyncratic and error-bespotted history of the town, *St Andrews*, his earliest history volume. He is buried by the east wall of the Eastern Cemetery abutting the cathedral precincts.

Andrew Greig the stentorian-voiced 'Starter' at the Old Course; the number '15' is the ballot number. The mobile starting box (used as tees were shifted) is probably a Victorian women's bathing machine for dressing on the beach. Greig, a blacksmith by trade, began his starting career in 1894 and continued it until his death on the Links in 1915. Special teeing grounds had only been started in 1877, the year players were required to 'replace turf'. By 1888 the Royal and Ancient had issued the *Rules of Golf* to all golf clubs, and when this photograph was taken (1894) the town had regained possession of the Links.

A group of caddies outside the Royal and Ancient Clubhouse, *c.* 1910. As the fishing trade declined in St Andrews, many of the fishermen became golf caddies. More often than not they retained their blue fishing jerseys and peaked caps, but this group have assumed a general working-class dress. Many of the caddies had nicknames like 'Boosey Chas', 'Stumpie Eye' and 'Kal Lad'.

A popular postcard view of the Royal and Ancient Clubhouse, the caddies' shed and the 1st and 18th holes of the Old Course, 1920s. The line of the railway sheds is seen in the distance, as are the wooded policies of Strathtyrum Estate. The water fountain by the mast is a memorial to Lyon Playfair, 1st Baron Playfair (1818–98), the cabinet-serving MP, scientist and courtier. The memorial was set up for the thrice-married peer by his children.

The LNER engine 9043, a North British Railway 4–4–2T C16 Class with guards van steams past the 16th green – 'The Corner of the Dyke Hole' – which contains the bunker known as the Principal's Nose. The occasion was one of the Amateur Championships of 1936. The railway line was constructed alongside the Links in 1851, after the Royal and Ancient successfully had it re-routed from plans which had it cutting through the 'Burn Hole'. The St Andrews–Leuchars line was closed to passengers on 6 January 1969.

Golf professional Laurie Ayton Jr's Children's Golf Class of 1948. He was selected as a Ryder Cup player in 1949. As old photographs show, children had been involved in golf from its early days and summer golf classes for children were popularised following the Second World War. In fact, the St Andrews Children's Golf Club was founded in 1888.

*Section Six*

# The Shutter Clicks on Various Scenes

*This print of Abbey Walk of 1846 is one of the early calotypes by the Scots pioneer photographers David Octavius Hill (1802–70) and Robert Adamson (1821–48). They made a set of twenty-two original calotypes for their album* A Series of Calotype Views of St Andrews *(1846). It shows a western stretch of the priory precinct wall reconstructed by Prior John Hepburn (d. 1522) and his successor and nephew, Prior Patrick Hepburn (d. 1537), Bishop of Moray. One of the thirteen attached towers is clearly seen. In the background is the corner house of Dauphin Hill (1786) and the row of Georgian houses (*c. *1813) at Greenside Place. Dauphin (once spelt 'Daupin') is from the local dyers' and launderers' process of dapping material.*

North Street seen from the tower of St Salvator's chapel looking east across the Fisher Quarter to the cathedral, before 1870. The roof of the Episcopal Church of St Andrew (1825–70; removed to Buckhaven) is seen in the foreground; the line of the Lang Riggs kitchen gardens parallel to North Castle Street is also clear.

George Cowie's picture of *c.* 1935 of the east end of South Street with the roundel (*c.* 1590), the now vanished gateway and buildings of the Priory mansion house, and the Abbey Bookshop, the latter being the site of Glass's Inn (until *c.* 1830), where James Boswell and Dr Samuel Johnson lodged in 1773. The bookshop's proprietor from 1931 until 1938 was J.H. Whyte.

J. Valentine's print, 1891, of the Cross Keys Hotel, Market Street, flanking Muttoe's Lane, with the Whyte-Melville memorial foundation to the right. There was a refronting of the building when it became an hotel in 1847.

William Ross's 1891 photograph of Joseph Cook's new bookshop at the junction of Market Street and Church Street. No. 80 Market Street was constructed in 1889 with no. 78 (opposite) dated 1873. By the junction there stood the burgh Mercat Cross, removed in 1768.

The south-western elevation of Holy Trinity Church before the rebuilding of 1907–9. The picture shows the church as built in 1789–99 on its 1412 foundation. From 1430 to 1749 the cemetery jutted south into the middle of modern South Street. By the west boundary railings stands the Mafeking Memorial (1900; now sited in Kinburn Park).

J. Valentine's popular mid-1950s postcard of Holy Trinity Church. The tower is all that remains of the church built here in 1412. Behind, by Logie's Lane, stands the Old City Hall (1845), built as the English School (1811) and later the Public Library of 1951.

Alexandra Place, *c.* 1910, with Hope Park Church (1864) and the Church Hall (1900) in the background. At the corner, opposite the church, was the Alexandra Hotel (then Station Hotel), which still has the old 'Blue Stane' – the whinstane 'boundary stone' – in its garden. By 1885 St Andrews was boasting the 'best street lighting in Scotland', following the replacement of oil lamps by town gas standards.

Children and servants pose in Queen Street (renamed Queen's Gardens in about 1896). Opened in 1858 at the time the new Scottish-gothic Town Hall of 1858–61 was begun, the street of fine town houses developed from 1858 to 1868, and sported individual architectural embellishments; gardens were developed from 1861 directly across the road from the houses.

Raphael Tuck & Son's postcard, in their 'Silverette' series, of North Street to the east of St Salvator's Chapel, *c.* 1910. To the right, between Alexander Braid's premises and Beethoven Lodge, is a now vanished vernacular fore-stair cottage. To the left stands Martyrs' Church (1843), modified in 1852, and rebuilt in 1929.

J. Valentine's photograph (*c.* 1878) of St Salvator's Collegiate Church, next to the corner tower house (71 North Street) of *c.* 1540 and flanked by Italian alders. The Collegiate Church (now the University Chapel) was built by Bishop James Kennedy in 1450–60, and a spire was added to the tower in about 1550. The western elevation building (73 North Street) by the tower is also of about 1450, with a storey added in 1687.

Market Street looking towards the west and Hope Park Church, *c.* 1945. The retail premises of Boyd's, Geddes's, McDougall's and Keracher's run along the left of the street, while on the far right is Woolworths (1935). Trees had been planted along Market Street in 1897 but were removed in 1936 at the request of Woolworths management.

A J. Valentine print of the east end of Market Street, *c.* 1896, looking towards the memorial fountain to the novelist George Whyte-Melville (1821–78). On the left, Mather's Waverley Temperance Hotel is seen at the corner of College Street, where the Central Bar is today.

Carts take rubbish and infill down to the West Sands, abutting The Scores, to construct the Bruce Embankment (*c.* 1893) on the wrecks of old fishing boats. The work was the inspiration of George Bruce (1825–1904), philanthropist, musician and poet.

Valentine's postcard, *c.* 1940, of Martyrs' Monument (1842), the Bandstand and the Royal and Ancient Clubhouse (1854) along The Scores. This area by the sea was popular from Victorian times for strolling, swimming (at The Step Rock) and skating; a skating rink was sited here from about 1875 to 1890.

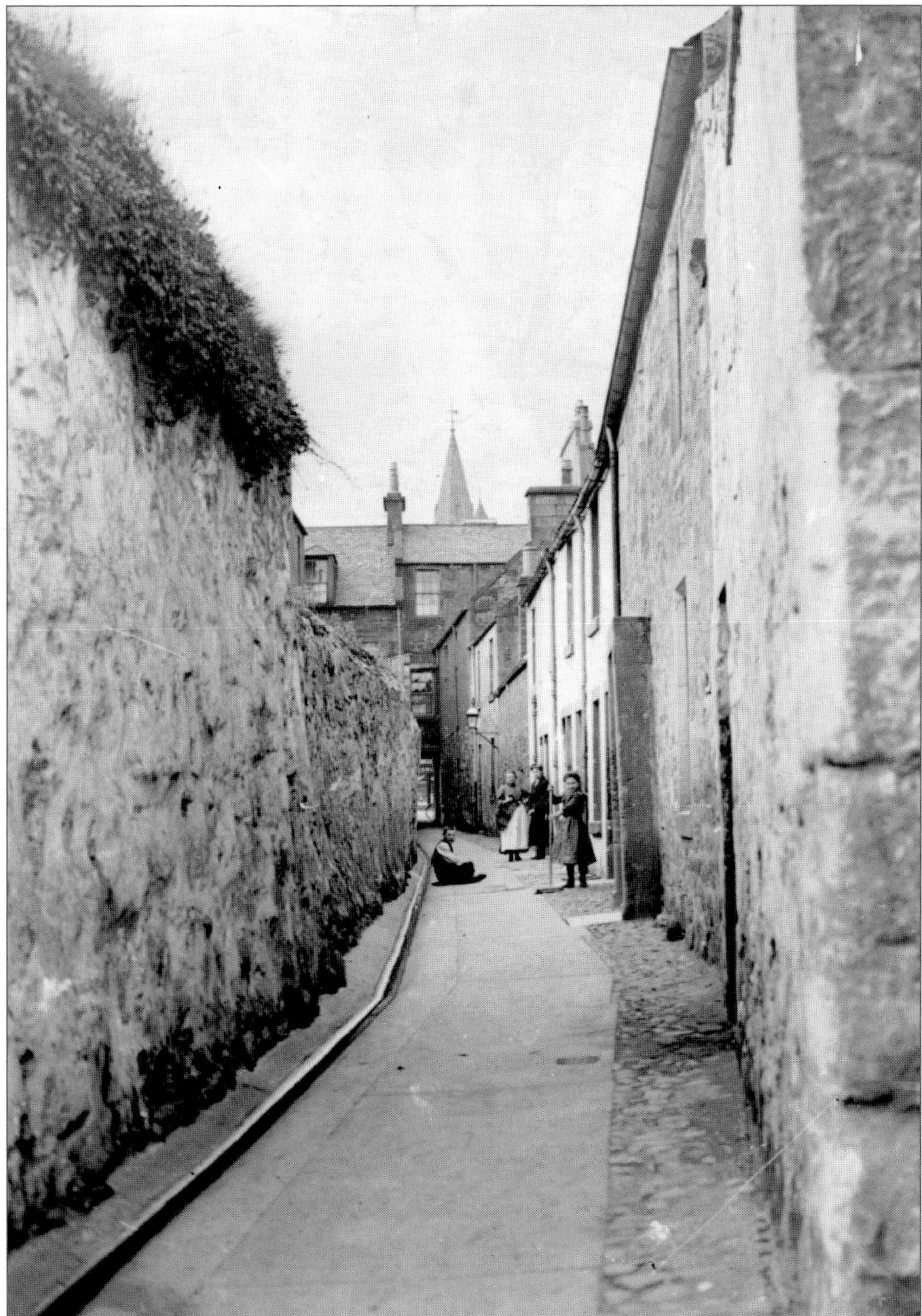

Muttoe's Lane (once Bakehouse Close), from the photograph by W. Patrick, looking south towards Market Street and the spire of Holy Trinity Church. Named after the family which included a former town clerk of the burgh, John Muttoe, some of the houses were built in part from stone salvaged from the ruined cathedral site, as the medieval masons' marks clearly show.

The unique and distinctive 'double decker' tenement town house at the corner of Market Street and Union Street, *c.* 1934. The house belonged to the Bruce family and was so named because of its double row of dormer windows in the roof. The house was demolished despite its architectural value by the Town Council's intensive campaign of pulling down 'old, sub-standard houses'.

George Fleming's postcard of South Castle Street – from the junction with Market Street – looking into North Castle Street with the spire of Castlegate House (1879) in the distance. Nos 13–15 show a traditional forestair and at no. 11 lived 'Joan', the last of St Andrews' fishwives.

George Washington Wilson's print (*c.* 1885) of the West Port looking east. Wilson (1823–93) was a popular topographical photographer who won a Royal Warrant in 1873. The semi-octagonal bastioned gateway was reconstructed in 1589 by the Blebo mason Thomas Robertson, who modelled it on the Edinburgh Netherbow Port. It was renovated between 1843 and 1845, when the side arches were inserted. The central plaque (1843) is of King David I and is the work of local mason Balfour Simmers.

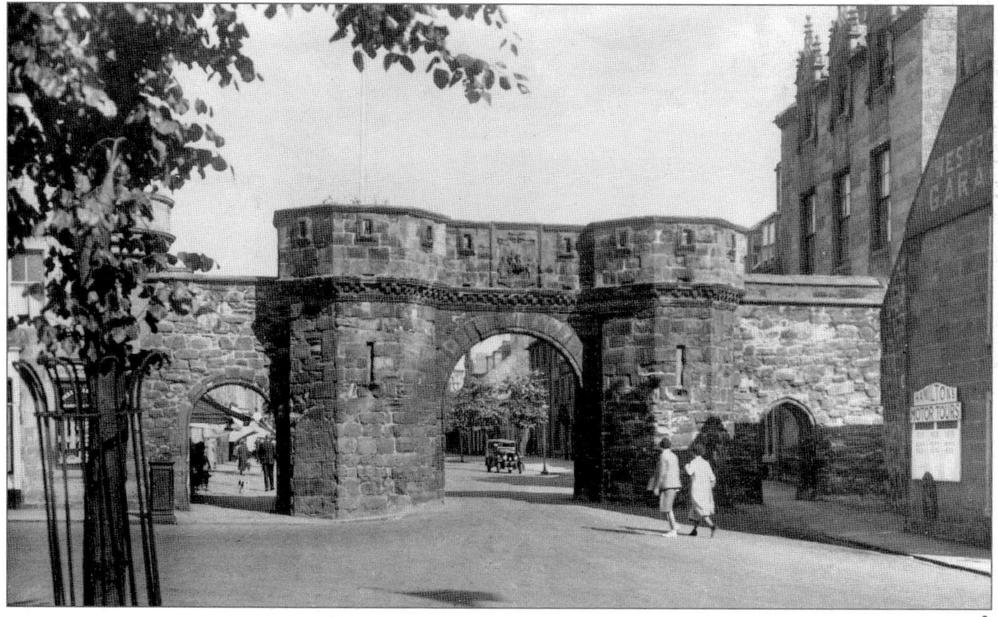


The West Port, *c.* 1940, and the West Port Garage. This remains the only surviving gateway into St Andrews. The latest renovation took place in 1950. In 1560 the West Port was known as the 'Argailles Port'. West Port House, here a part of the garage, was demolished in 1969.

Thomas Rodger's print of the cathedral ruins, *c.* 1865. Founded in 1160, and consecrated by Bishop William de Lamberton in the presence of King Robert I, the Bruce, in 1318, the cathedral had an internal length of 357 ft. The south nave wall, and that of the south transept, seen here, dates from 1160–*c.* 1200. The figure is sitting on a central tomb set in the old choir. During 1826 the ruins of the cathedral had been taken over by the Barons of the Exchequer and excavated; interments ceased in the nave in 1834. The original sites of the pillars of the cathedral nave and the lines of demolished walls were set out in the turf in 1888. The chapter house (extreme left) was excavated in 1904–5.

This 1947 print shows the line of the medieval streets fanning west from the cathedral site. The Shorehead houses by the harbour were rebuilt in 1965–66 as houses and flats. The sluice of 1787 was augmented by a footbridge over the inner harbour entrance in 1925. To the left the gasometer of 1903 can be seen on the site of the Royal Tennis Courts, which gave way to the tennis courts of St Leonards School (founded in 1877). From the medieval Mill Port gateway, the school buildings up Pends Road are the Sanatorium (1899), the Hospice (1894), St Rules (1895–96) and College Hall (1868; later Bishopshall). At the mid-left, the medieval Lang Riggs are clearly seen running south from South Street.

Cattle make their way up Largo Road to Ireland's farm at Claybraes, *c.* 1934. The chimneys of the electricity station are seen above the houses on the left. The town had many dairy farms within its bounds, including those at Claybraes, Argyll Farm, Alley Place, Westburn Lane and Kinnessburn Road.

Melbourne Brae, looking north, at the junction with Bridge Street and Kinnessburn Road, *c.* 1910. Here the road crosses 'Maggie Murray's Bridge', named by rather dubious local legend after Margaret Murray – daughter of William Murray, landowner at the Bassaguard (Bess Acre) from 1767 and of the land at Wal Wynde (Well Wynd) – who paid for its construction. Well Wynd was re-named Bridge Street in 1843.

Melbourne Brae, looking south, *c.* 1910 – with Kinness Place (left) and Melbourne Place (right), as they were known from 1895. The 'Melbourne' is from the Australian connections of the ground feuer of the area, Alexander Herd.

The romantically high Victorian 'Westerlee', Kennedy Gardens, *c.* 1865, showing the cultivated land to the north and west now covered by the North Haugh campus and residences of the university. 'Westerlee', now part of University Hall (opened 1896 as the first residence for women), was the work of architect John Milne (1823–1904). The house is a significant example of the Victorian western expansion of St Andrews, and the owners' desire to take advantage of the spectacular views of the Eden Estuary and the Sidlaw Hills.

A beautifully posed picture of the then already derelict water-wheel at Law Mill, *c.* 1900. Once belonging to the Augustinian Priory, the Law Mill was probably founded in the thirteenth century and came to be owned by the burgh by 1660. It was privately owned by 1848.

John McHardy, butcher and family, survey their cows at the now built-on site at Lade Braes. The houses of the Lade Braes were developed from 1895. Mc Hardy's butcher's shop was in Kinnessburn Road.

The Law Mill, Law Park. The lades of the Lumbo Burn and the Kinnessburn fed the Law Mill dam. A new artificial pond was constructed at Law Mill in 1905.

*SECTION SEVEN*

# JUST ENTERTAINMENT

*Wooden bathing machines lined up on the West Sands in this George Washington Wilson picture of* c. *1888, when Victorian St Andrews had fully emerged as a popular seaside resort. The line of The Scores, developed from about 1810, runs across the north-facing clifftop overlooking the West Sands, revealing in the roadway's name its origins in the Old Norse word* sker *(a cliff top). From right to left can be seen: The Martyr's Monument (1842); the 'Tin Tabernacle' Catholic church (1885); 'Rockview' and 'Northcliff' (1863); University House (1863–65); 'Edgecliff' (1864–66); 'Kirnan'* (c. *1866); and 'Castlecliff'* (c. *1877) – leading the eye to the castle ruins and Kirkhill. The gaily painted bathing machines were trundled in and out of the sea by horsepower, led for many years by one Maggie Stark; the machines remained until the mid-1930s.*

The popular 'Pierrots' Theatre' company pose for this *c.* 1920s shot. Such pierrot shows had been introduced from France in the 1890s. These companies played both the East and West Sands.

Racing taking place at the larger of the sea-filled pools of the Step Rock complex in the late 1930s. The sunbathing tiers of the pool areas were an innovation patronised throughout the year.

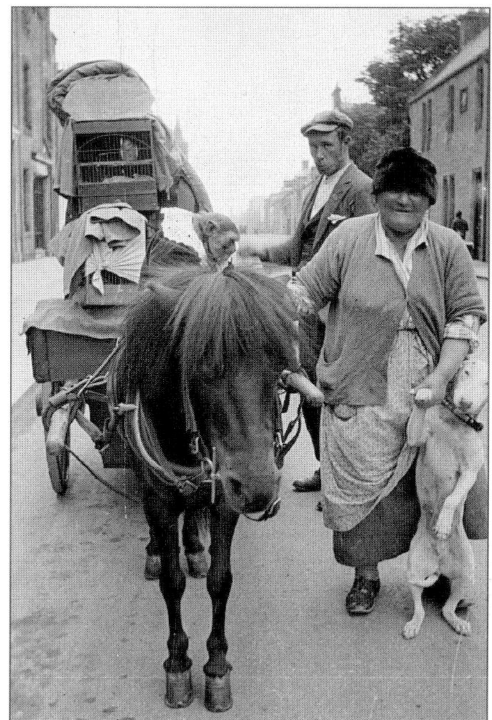

Angela Varecchi and partner, itinerant street entertainers, pose in Ellice Place, North Street, *c.* 1935. They toured the streets with their cacophonous barrel organ, performing monkey and 'fortune telling' lovebirds at the time of the Lammas Market. They lived in Edinburgh's Grassmarket.

Bill Wilson clowns it up in the George V Silver Jubilee procession of 6 May 1935. From Buckingham Palace the king broadcast the message: 'I dedicate myself anew to your service for all the years that may still be left to me.' He died on 20 January 1936.

When the circus came to St Andrews clowns and animals often paraded round the streets. Here an elephant pays a call at Macgregor's and the next door Central Bar, Market Street, in the 1950s.

A street market by the Whyte-Melville Memorial fountain (right) and outside the Cross Keys Hotel, Market Street, *c.* 1919. The trees, now removed, date from 1897.

Roller-skating was very much an Edwardian craze, although the four-wheeled roller skate was invented in America in 1863. Here a group of St Andrews enthusiasts enjoy the facilities at the newly opened rink at James Street; the bunting is celebrating the coronation of King George V on 22 June 1911. In 1909 a local contractor, John D. Spence, bought the old Roman Catholic church – the 'Tin Tabernacle' – and transported it to James Street. The wood and corrugated-iron building was used as a cinema, a rink and for other leisure purposes.

Fairfield Stores Annual Summer Outing, *c.* 1914; the employees pose in the sixteenth-century South Range Courtyard of Falkland Palace. The Fairfield Stores (St Andrews) Ltd was long a prominent drapers and outfitters at 68–72 Market Street. Staff outings in general became more popular as the railway system developed.

St Andrews Cycling Club at the inner entrance of Archbishop John Hamilton's entrance gateway to the courtyard of St Andrews castle. The year is 1897, and the club was holding a rally to celebrate Queen Victoria's Diamond Jubilee.

Alexander Brown Paterson (1907–89), playwright and freelance journalist, surveys the old Abbey Street Dairy Farm byre, where the St Andrews Play Club founded the famous Byre Theatre in 1933. The picture, by Tad Kucharski, shows the Byre before its demolition in 1969 to make way for the new theatre. Alex Paterson led the founder members and was administrator of the theatre for over forty years.

The cramped conditions of the Old Byre Theatre are seen in this performance of the 1951 season of R.J.B. Sellar's play based on Sir Walter Scott's *Heart of Midlothian*. Here Margaret Watson (as Jeanie Deans), supported by Eric N. Smith (as pastor Reuben Butler), prepares to plead for her sister's life to Queen Caroline (Patricia Brake).

The autumn hiring fair of Lammas Market, South Street, *c.* 1900, taken from the West Port. The oldest continually held market in Scotland, the Lammas hirings of agricultural workers mostly took place outside the Royal Hotel (middle distance); the hotel closed in 1963 and the *c.* 1815 building became the university's Southgait Hall.

The town band play for dancing at the Lammas Market in Logies Lane, *c.* 1911. The main building shown is the old City Hall of 1845, which was later redeveloped as the Public Library. The band played for pennies from the crowd; when they had enough they would retire to a local hostelry for refreshment. As the day went on, and the beer flowed, their playing became more and more eccentric.

Members of the St Andrews Curling Club discuss the lie of the curling stones at a rink at the Lawmill Curling Pond, *c.* 1925. The club was founded in 1846. By 1854 it was renting a pond from the Cheapes of Strathtyrum, and in 1905 the artificial pond was laid out at Lawmill.

W. Macdonald delivers a stone and A.C. Muirhead looks on at the opening of the Burnside Pond, by St Andrews, on 8 January 1931. By the late 1930s indoor rinks had begun to be built.

St Andrews curlers G.A. Geddes and W. Boyd take up a classic stance watched by J. Mackie and R. Robertson at Lawmill Pond, January 1934.

The lunch break: four St Andrews curlers pose with brushes and wickerwork curling-stone baskets in 1931 at the opening of the Burnside Pond. From left to right: J.E. Bett, G.L. Munro, W.H. Lawson, and A.G. Scott.

*Section Eight*

# People on Parade

*Provost Moir leads 'Kate Kennedy' (Bejant Macgregor) back to her carriage after the official reception at the Town Hall, 17 April 1954. The St Andrews University Kate Kennedy Club is a society which organises various charity events and promotes the colourful 'Kate Kennedy Day' procession each spring, depicting characters from the history of Town and Gown. 'Kate' is traditionally played by a male first year student (a bejant). Jessie Love Moir (1893–1987) was the first and only woman Provost (cf. English mayor) of St Andrews, 1952–55; she had been co-opted as a member of the Town Council in 1942. The town's first female councillor was Frances Jane Warrack (1864–1950).*

Town Officer Alex Petrie leads Provost W.P.A. Tulloch and Town Clerk Neil Mackenzie during the procession of Sunday, 8 May 1949, to the church service at Holy Trinity Church, known as the 'Kirking of the Council'. Behind come baillies Andrew Thom; Jessie Moir; Thomas Livingstone; and Jack Anderson, followed by members of the Town Council and council officials.

Provost W.P.A. Tulloch reads the loyal address to HM Queen Elizabeth on her visit to St Andrews on Wednesday, 20 September 1950, with members of the Town Council standing to the rear. The Town Clerk, Neil Mackenzie, holds the address box and the Earl of Elgin, Lord Lieutenant of Fife, and Sheriff Principal Lillie, stand to the right.

Captain David Lamb prepares to line up the men of the 3rd Fife Artillery Volunteers (founded *c.* 1883) in a photograph of *c.* 1890. They stand by the gun battery set opposite the Signal Station, Kirkhill. Behind can be seen the 1849 'White Lantern, Turret Light' on a tower of Prior Hepburn's medieval walls. St Andrews Foundry is off centre by the Fisher School of 1856.

Men of the Highland Cycle Battalion (with BSA folding bicycles) line up outside Liddel & Smith Builders, and the Templars Hall (*c.* 1890), North Street, 1914. The Templars Hall (owned until 1966 by the Order of the Eastern Star) stood where the south entrance to the University Library is now. To the left are the St Katherine's School buildings (bought 1894), now the area of the Crawford Centre.

A. Downie's portrait of the local volunteer NCOs, men and drummer boys of the Artillery Company and the Rifle Corps, posed at the east wing of Madras College, 1860. The volunteers had the use of the college rooms and grounds for their drill.

Ratings, NCOs and bandsmen of the British Channel Fleet walk down Kirkhill to the harbour, *c.* 1910. The Royal Navy regularly 'laid off' the East Neuk during these days. The car to the left displays the early Fife registration number SP 4.

W. Patrick's view of the gathering to hear the proclamation of the accession of the forty-four-year-old King George V, following the death of his father Edward VII just before midnight on Friday, 6 May 1910. Provost John Wilson (served 1908–11) presides near the site of the burgh's medieval Mercat Cross.

Town Clerk N.C.H. Mackenzie reads the proclamation of Queen Elizabeth II at the site of the Mercat Cross, 15 February 1952. Councillors Humphries, Cowan, Niven, Armit, Frazer, Caithness and Fordyce stand behind Provost Tulloch, with Dean of Guild Meiklejohn, Baillies Thom and Miss Moir.

St Andrews Brass Band leads the annual walk of the burgh's masons, *c.* 1914. There was a lodge of freemasons in St Andrews as early as 1600, but the current Lodge 25 dates from the 1720s.

HRH the Duchess of York walks with headmistress Miss Katherine Howard McCutcheon (1876–1956) during the royal visit to St Leonards School on 1 October 1927 for the school's fiftieth Jubilee celebrations. The duchess opened the new school library at Queen Mary's House. Behind walks the Rt Revd C.E. Plumb, Episcopal Bishop of St Andrews, Dunkeld and Dunblane, Chairman of the School Council from 1924 to 1930.

HM Queen Elizabeth the Queen Mother visits St Leonards School to open the new science block and gymnasium in October 1962. She greets former headmistress (1938–55) Dr Janet Macfarlane, watched by the then headmistress Dr Janet Macauley (retired 1970), and the Queen's Extra Woman of the Bedchamber, Lady Victoria Wemyss (1890–1994) – the last surviving godchild of Queen Victoria.

An academic procession past St Salvator's College. The four university janitors carry a selection of the university maces. The occasion was the 500th anniversary of the foundation of the College of St Salvator, 20–21 September 1950. Behind the maces come Sir James Irvine, Principal and Vice-Chancellor of the University of St Andrews; the Duke of Hamilton, Chancellor; Albany Herald, Sir Francis Grant; and HM Queen Elizabeth.

Induction of Professor (later Sir) Thomas Malcolm Knox as Principal and Vice-Chancellor of the University of St Andrews, 20 November 1953. Left to right (front row): Lord Provost Black of Dundee; Provost Jessie Moir of St Andrews; Earl of Crawford and Balcarres; Earl of Elgin, Lord Lieutenant of Fife; the Duke of Hamilton and Brandon, Chancellor of the university.

Sir Wilfred Thomason Grenfell (1865–1940), physician and missionary, arrives at St Andrews station for his installation as Rector of the University of St Andrews, November 1928. Elected triannually by the students, the Rector is their representative and chairs the University Court; the office dates from 1411.

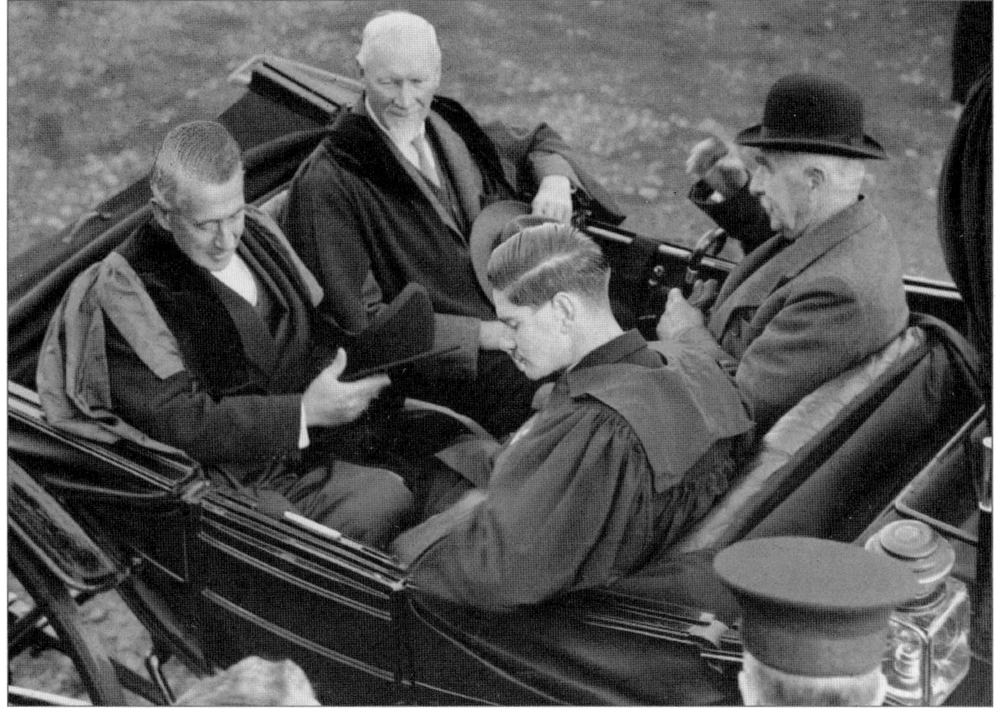

University Principal and Vice-Chancellor, Sir James Irvine, sits next to Jan Christian Smuts (1870–1950) – South African Prime Minister (1939) – on the occasion of his installation as Rector of the university in 1931. Also in the carriage is the SRC representative and Dr William Low, Rector's Assessor.

The staff of St Andrews University process down Gregory's Green (North Street) as a part of the funeral cortège of Principal Sir James Donaldson (1831–1915). Donaldson was Principal of the United College at St Andrews from 1886 to 1890, and in 1890 he became the first holder of the new office of Principal of the University until his death. A classical scholar, Donaldson promoted the Education Act of 1872 which established compulsory primary education in Scotland.

Bandmaster James Auchterlonie (seated fifth from the left) led the music of the St Andrews City Brass Band on the occasion of the Coronation Sports at University Park, Hepburn Gardens, 22 June 1911.

Provost John Reid, with the Principal of St Andrews University, Sir James Irvine and Town Clerk, J. Cargill Cantley, addresses the assembled company at the unveiling of the commemorative plaque presented by Polish soldiers to the citizens of St Andrews on 21 October 1941. The work of soldiers Wlodzimierz Klocek, Jan Sterling and Ewaryst Jakubowski, the plaque was unveiled by General Paszkiewicz who stands near the Provost with interpreter Siemiatkowski.

Crowds gather outside the old post office, 101–3 South Street, to read the posted up casualty lists during the Boer War (1899–1902). The building had been custom-built as a post office in 1892; the premises became the Christian Institute from 1907 to 1963.

The Cottage Hospital (cost £3,000) was opened on Wednesday, 27 August 1902. The photograph, by J. Fairweather, taken a short time after the official opening, shows left to right: (seated) Alexander Thoms (benefactor of the children's ward); Matron, Miss Torrence; Dr John Wilson Moir (1843–1926), Medical Officer of the Hospital; and Nurse Scott. Left to right: (standing) Nurse Legge; Dr William Butterworth MacTier (d. 1933), Hon. Medical Officer; and an unknown nurse.

*Section Nine*

# A Place to Work

*Malcolm Patterson works at a John Haddon & Co. hand-printing press, c. 1925. Alexander Wilson (1714–86) was born in St Andrews, and is known in printing history as the 'Father of Scottish Letter Founding'. Wilson and another St Andrean, John Bain, entered into partnership and set up a type foundry in 1742 at the corner of Church Street and South Street (where the Citizen Bookshop is now). John Bain established in 1787 the first type-foundry in Philadelphia, Pennsylvania, USA, and in 1797 his firm cast the first dollar sign ever used in America.*

Rural and town postmen and telegraphic staff at St Andrews post office at 101–3 South Street, just before the First World War. The post office was built here in 1892 and was moved to 127 South Street (its

position today) in 1907; up to 1862 a post office was sited at 7 Union Street. During the eighteenth century the university operated its own postal system.

Foreman Tom Black supervises the re-tarmacadamising of Alfred Place at the point where it merges with Alexandra Place near the (now demolished) Volunteer Hall. The squad employed by Burgh Surveyor William Watson's department endeavours to combat the 'dust nuisance' of the 'motor season'.

A. Downie's photograph of the staff of St Andrews gasworks, after 1900. The gasworks was constructed by the east precinct wall of the Priory of St Andrews (the top of the 'Inscription Tower' can be seen above the roof, left) in 1835 and demolished in 1964. The St Andrews Gas Co. ceased to exist after 1949 when it was taken over by the Gas Board.

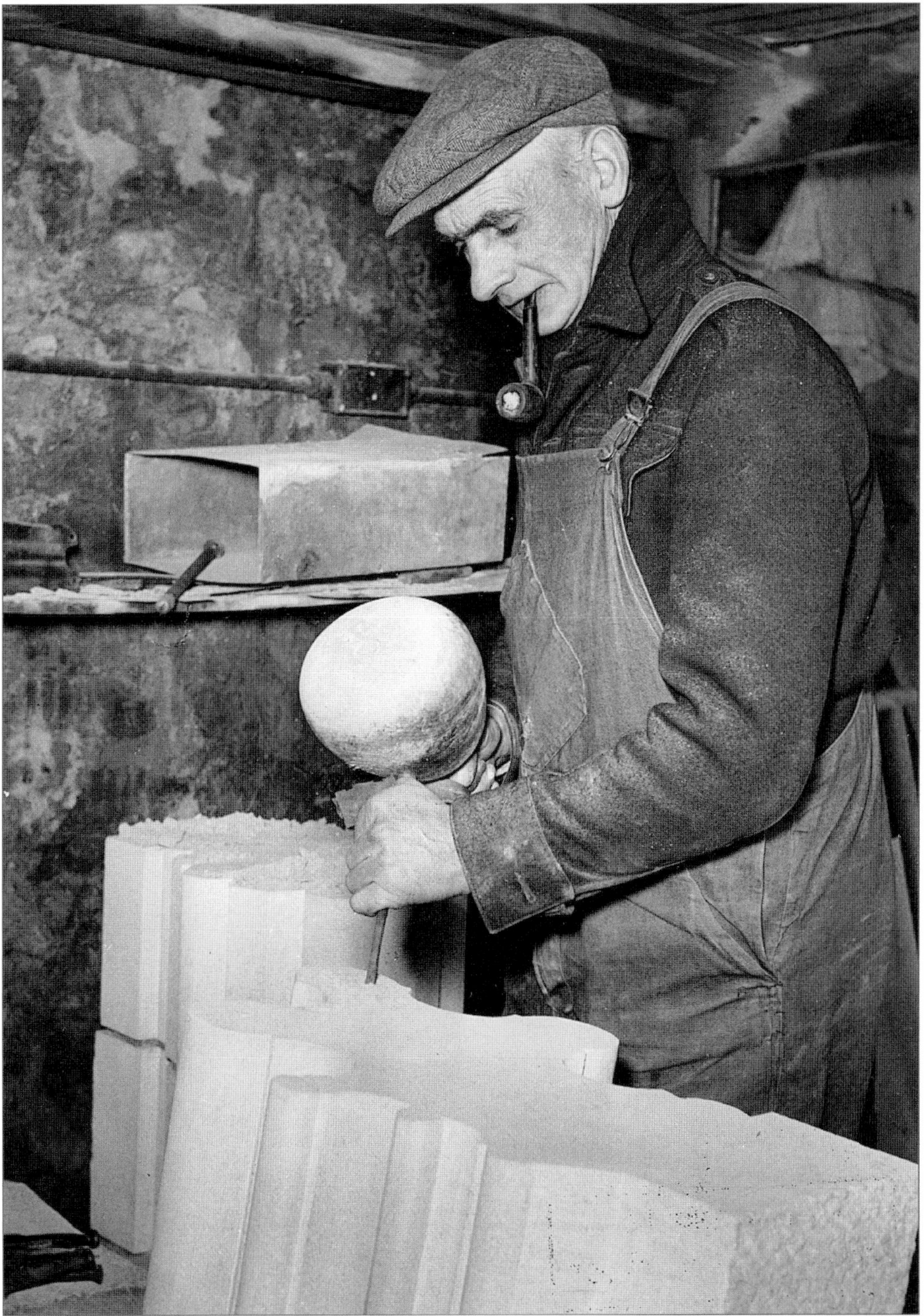

Robert 'Bob' Taylor, mason with F.D. Baillie & Co., 64 Argyll Street, working on replacement stone for the arched, gothic tomb of James Kennedy (1408–68), Bishop of St Andrews, founder of St Salvator's College (1450). The tomb was placed in the college chapel before Kennedy's death.

Staff of D.S. Ireland's Brewery. The eighteenth-century premises contained one of the deepest wells in St Andrews and produced premier grade water of mineral content; it was re-bored in 1886 to 225.5 feet. The brewery premises were taken over by John Wilson's Bottling Co. Ltd. The site is now executive sheltered flats.

A. Watney's demonstration vehicle and company delivery lorry at John Wilson's Bottling Co. Ltd, Argyll Street. The beer and mineral water company began trading at Market Street in 1876 and moved to Argyll Street in 1906. The company ceased trading on 31 December 1984. Owner John Wilson (1854–1938), was Provost of St Andrews from 1908 to 1911.

James Lamb, hairdresser and perfumier, with staff at his premises at 106 South Street, photographed by A. Downie, *c.* 1900. The premises were later taken over by George Clow, who advertised 'special attention is given to the Cutting and Trimming of Children's Hair' – and, in the days of rampant head lice, he boasted 'antiseptics are ever in use'.

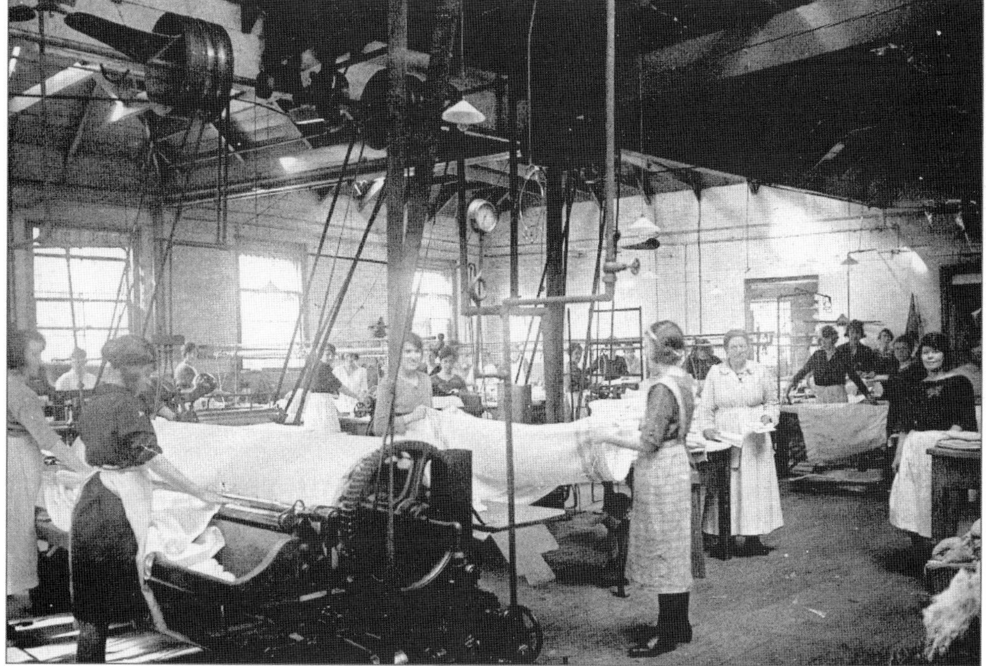

Fairweather's photograph of the ironing-room of the Woodburn Steam Laundry (formerly the St Leonard's Laundry and Supply Co. Ltd), whose collection depot was at 99 Market Street. Coal fires and street grime made laundering a high priority on a family's budget in St Andrews of yesteryear.

Jock Graham, Martin Czerajewski and Tommy Corstorphine work on the production of turnip seeders at Greenside Works, Queens Terrace. Known as 'The St Andrews Improved Seeder', the implement won a medal at the Fife Agricultural Show of 1951.

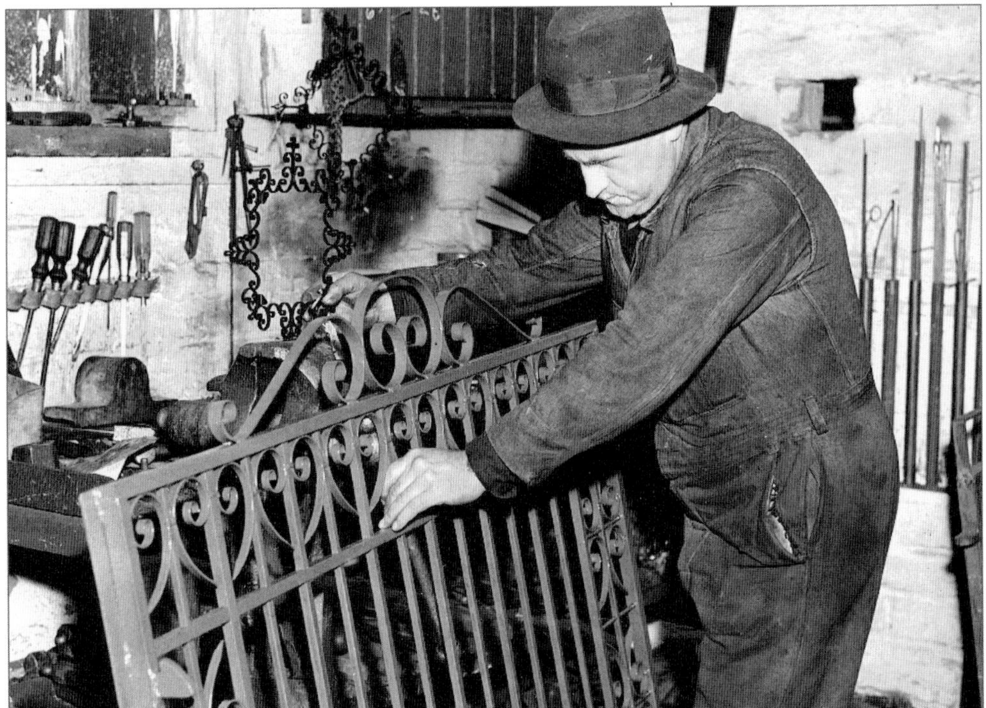

Edward P. Harvey (1907–85), master farrier and blacksmith, at Greenside Works, where he ran his ironworks business from 1949 to 1984. His work still graces the town's gardens, courtyards and buildings, and he is remembered too as farrier for Woodburn Riding Stables and the beach donkeys.

Nisbet, taxi driver for Tommy Methven, checks the pump at the Royal Hotel, South Street. In this year (*c.* 1949), BP petrol cost 1*s* 7*d* including 9*d* tax. The Royal Hotel closed in 1963 and the property became the university residence of Southgait Hall.

The Smoking Room of Rusack's Marine Hotel, *c.* 1906. Other facilities advertised were 'Winter Gardens, Private Suites with bathrooms and Electric Lift'; by then the hotel boasted two telephones and the leading accommodation in the 'Ideal Climate for Winter Golf'.

The reconstruction of the front entrance to Rusack's Marine Hotel, Pilmour Links elevation. The Rusack family acquired the land here in 1884. The houses to the right were later demolished to give access to the hotel kitchens; and then to new flats in the 1990s.

Early stylised advertising drawing of Rusack's Marine Hotel at The Links, by the 1st and 18th of the Old Course. The hotel was founded by Johann Wilhelm Christof Rusack (1848–1916), a native of Bad Halrzburg, Lower Saxony. Soon after he came to St Andrews in 1874 he started up 'Rusack's Private Hotel', Abbotsford Crescent. The Marine Hotel was opened in 1887, and enlarged in 1892 and 1894. The hotel was much patronised by royalty and famous golfers. The family also owned Bogward Farm which became Rusack's Home Farm. The hotel was acquired by the St Andrews Links Trust in 1980 and by Forte International in 1985, to be absorbed into the Granada group in 1996.

Delivery vans outside George Bowman, butcher, and Andrew Keracher, fishmonger, 108 Market Street in the late 1920s; to the right (across the pend) Murray Mitchell, butcher, who succeeded Robertson's chemists in 1926. The firm of Andrew Keracher, purveyors of poultry, fish and game (shop established 1924) closed in 1996, but Murray Mitchell's is still in existence.

Robert Pratt, butcher and poulterer, 66 Market Street by Croil's Lane, was established in the 1870s. By the 1890s, when this picture was taken, the shop was one of the most prominent purveyors of meat in the St Andrews area.

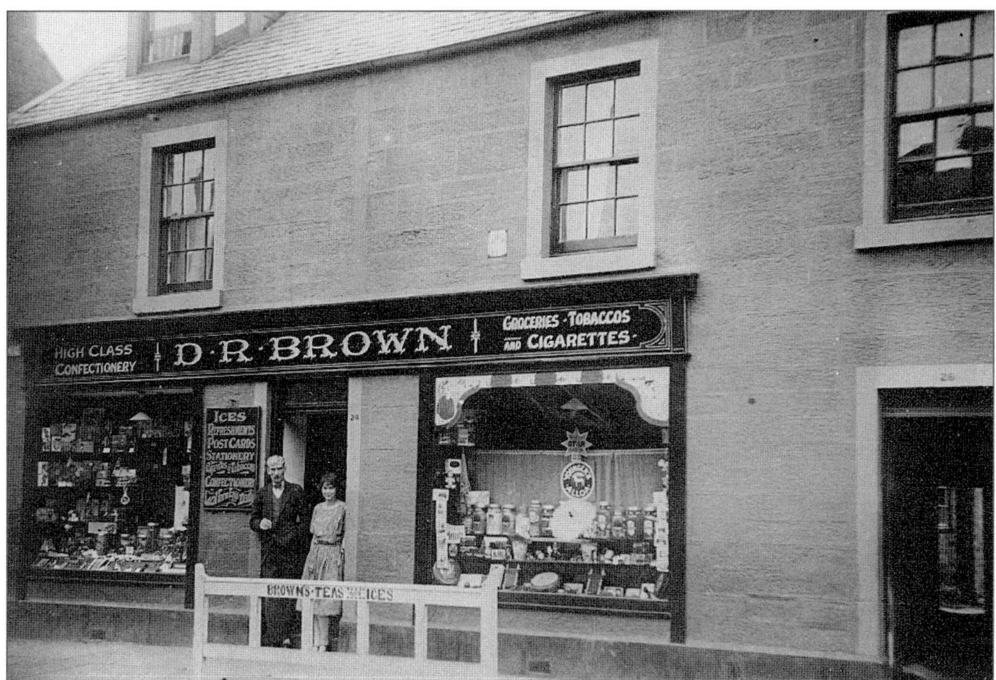


David Brown and his daughter Letitia stand outside their shop, D.R. Brown, grocer, stationer, tobacconist and confectioner, 24 North Street. This shop had the reputation of being open 364 days a year; the premises are now a tea shop.

Once a professional golfer, the characterful and stentorian-voiced Robert B. 'Buff' Wilson poses on the steps of his newsagent's shop at 206 South Street in 1921. Displayed are his sets of second-hand golf-clubs, which he sold from 2*s* 6*d* upwards .

Sawmill workers at the Robert Forgan works, 1891. Robert Forgan (1824–1900), golf-club and ball maker, learned his trade from the celebrated clubmaker Hugh Philp (1728–1856); Forgan took over Philp's business in 1856. Set at The Links, St Andrews, the firm of R. Forgan & Son were to win an international reputation as craftsmen.

D. Anderson's workshop, by Ellice Place. This photograph by Fairweather shows the large staff retained to satisfy the golf market then picking up after the First World War. St Andrews clubmakers like Stewart, Condie, Anderson and Forgan (all now defunct) were the world's leaders for craftsmanship.

Croft-an-Righ Farm, Argyle Street (opposite Double Dykes Road), photographed by J. Fairweather, *c.* 1900. The farm belonged to the Louden family and its name is thought by some historians to be a modern adjustment of Croftangry, itself from the Latin *crofta ankeri*, 'the hermit's cell', the dwelling of a medieval dependant of the Priory of St Andrews, which owned lands here in medieval times.

The removal of the last Toll Bar from Argyll Street at the burgh's western limits. In the photograph are Major John Bell (Pilmour Links); Donald Rose (Louden's Close); Andrew Young, Town Inspector and Burgh Surveyor; and County Road Surveyor Gatherum.

The staff and family of John McHardy, butcher and poulterer, Kinnessburn Road. Opposite Fleming Place, the site is now a betting shop. The consumption of meat was always a sensitive indicator of living standards, and the growth of specialist butchers in the burgh between the 1880s and 1914 was a reliable judge of improvement.

John G. Petrie's Cabinet & Upholstery Warehouse, 7 Greyfriars Garden. The firm also acted as house agents and property appraisers. The staff in the photograph included Petrie's carpenters, upholstery finishers and cabinet makers. The influx of prosperous middle-class families to St Andrews in Victoria's later years provided much trade for the town's furniture craftsmen.

*SECTION TEN*

# FRIENDLY NEIGHBOURS

*Earlshall castle from the west barmkin wall, with picnic group, c. 1870. The sixteenth-century L-plan tower house was begun by Sir William Bruce (1486–1584) in 1546. The building was restored by Sir Robert Stodart Lorimer (1864–1925) between 1891 and 1898, for the then owner Robert Mackenzie, a bleach merchant of Dundee. The gateway barmkin wall, seen here, links the tower house with the seventeenth-century range which formed the former coachman's house and stables, across an entrance courtyard. The castle remains one of the most complete examples in Fife of a late sixteenth-century grouping of house and ancillary buildings around a small courtyard. The building was never a place of defence – despite the loopholes and arrow slits – and was more the baronial residence of a local magnate than the feudal castle of a warlike baron.*

Margaret Maul (right, who died aged 103) watches sister-maids drawing water from Earlshall castle courtyard well in 1892. To the right is the strangely named building Dummy Daws, said to have been so called after an eighteenth-century coachman who was dumb.

Thompson the gardener holds the head of the Shetland pony drawing the castle lawnmower at Earlshall, 1920s. Seen here are some of the thirty-six topiary yews (brought by Sir Robert Lorimer from a disused Edinburgh garden), planted to form four saltires (St Andrew's crosses, X shapes).

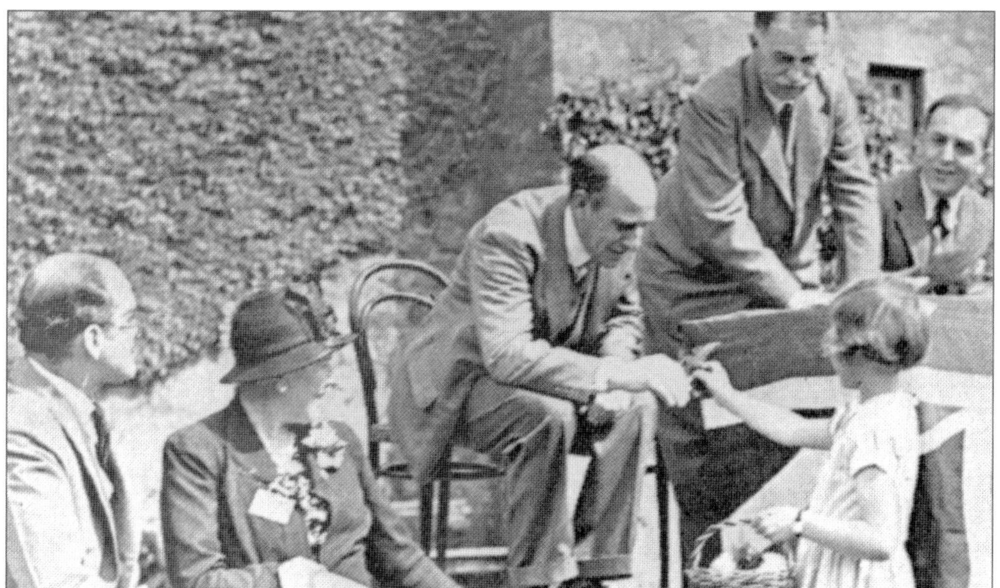

The National Government Fête at Earlshall, 1 July 1939. Margaret Walker presents a buttonhole to National Liberal MP, Leslie Burgin, Minister of Supply. Coalition National Governments served the UK from August 1931 to 1945. In the photograph are young Margaret's grandparents Sir Michael and Lady Nairn and (later Sir) John Henderson-Stewart, National Liberal and Conservative MP for East Fife (1933–61).

A rare aerial photograph of Leuchars village, just before the air display of 25 May 1935. The now defunct Leuchars (Old) station (closed to passengers in 1921) is seen at the bottom of the picture; the station and line site is now covered by the A919 road extension.

Ed Harvey (right), who was to become a well-known St Andrews farrier and blacksmith, stands outside the long-vanished Erskine's Smiddy at Leuchars, *c.* 1925. The wooden rounds on which they have placed bands were from trees on Earlshall Estate.

During the Second World War Leuchars airbase was linked to St Andrews coastal/land defence interests by a radio telegraph service manned by observers. In this picture, dating from 1942, Chief Observer Keith tests lines with Observers Braid and Meldrum.

Leuchars village, *c.* 1925. Centre right stands the parish church of St Athernase, at Schoolhill, built in 1183–7. Once the village was made up of two knoll sites – Castle Knowe, where stood the mid-eighteenth-century demolished Norman castle, and Temple Hill, the centre of the modern village – surrounded by marshes. In about 1790 Sir David Carnegie ordered the construction of a Great Drain which dried the marshes, and the village of 'Lochyeords' evolved. To the east of the church in Earlshall Road is the whinstone manse (1803–5), while the mostly single-storey, pantiled houses seen around the church are mainly of the late eighteenth and early nineteenth century. On the sward to the south of the church is the new medical centre.

Hangars at the 'Technical End' of Leuchars airbase, *c.* 1926. Royal Engineers carried out experiments with balloons here in 1911 and the Royal Navy established a Fleet Training School at Leuchars during 1914–18. The RAF Station was established on 20 March 1920 for 203 and 205 squadrons.

Leuchars airbase looking towards the village, *c.* 1925. By this date 443 and 444 (Fleet Reconnaissance) Flights worked out of Leuchars. The base became a part of Coastal Command in 1936, with a retention of naval training, which was to last until 1978 when 892 Naval Air Squadron departed.

A 3F (S.1213) lies on its nose after a mishap at the sick bay at RAF Leuchars in 1928. Around this time pilots were trained at Leuchars on working mock-ups to deal with being catapulted off the turrets of capital ships. Landings were not always guaranteed upright.

A DH9A (biplane H.3523) lands on its nose to the east of Leuchars (Milton Junction) station, *c.* 1927. These were the days when crews were being trained at Leuchars for 'naval spotting' from capital ships.

A Sopwith Snipe at Leuchars, mid-1920s. Leuchars had seen many 'string and sealing wax' aircraft of the embryo Royal Flying Corps, and many planes took off and landed at St Andrews West Sands; fuel obtained at local garages was an important local back-up service.

A Parnall Panther (N,7521) outside one of the original (and still existing) hangars at Leuchars airbase. During the 1920s the base hosted Parnall Panthers, Nieuport Nighthawks, Fairey IIIDs and Flycatchers, all involved in reconnaissance, spotting and aerial combat programmes.

'Bomb Dump Wallahs', Leuchars, May 1943. Ranges for practice bombing had already been established at nearby Tentsmuir Forest in 1935. No. 3 Armament Practice Corps operated here from 1942, with air to ground firing, bombing and rocket projectile firing practice carried out at Tentsmuir.

Riggers and Wireless Operators with bomber 'F for Freddie' at Leuchars in the 1940s. In 1941, 42 Squadron (Beauforts) and 107 Squadron (Blenheims) flew out of Leuchars to carry out anti-shipping sweeps, convoy escorts, and to bomb Norwegian ports and airfields, and to make coastal defence sorties; they also conducted general reconnaissance patrols.

A Flycatcher with maintenance crew at Leuchars, 1920s. By 1925 Leuchars had three training flights: A-Flight Training, B-Spotter Training, and C-Reconnaissance. The fighter flights were equipped with Flycatchers, while reconnaissance flights had Fairey IIIDs and Panthers.

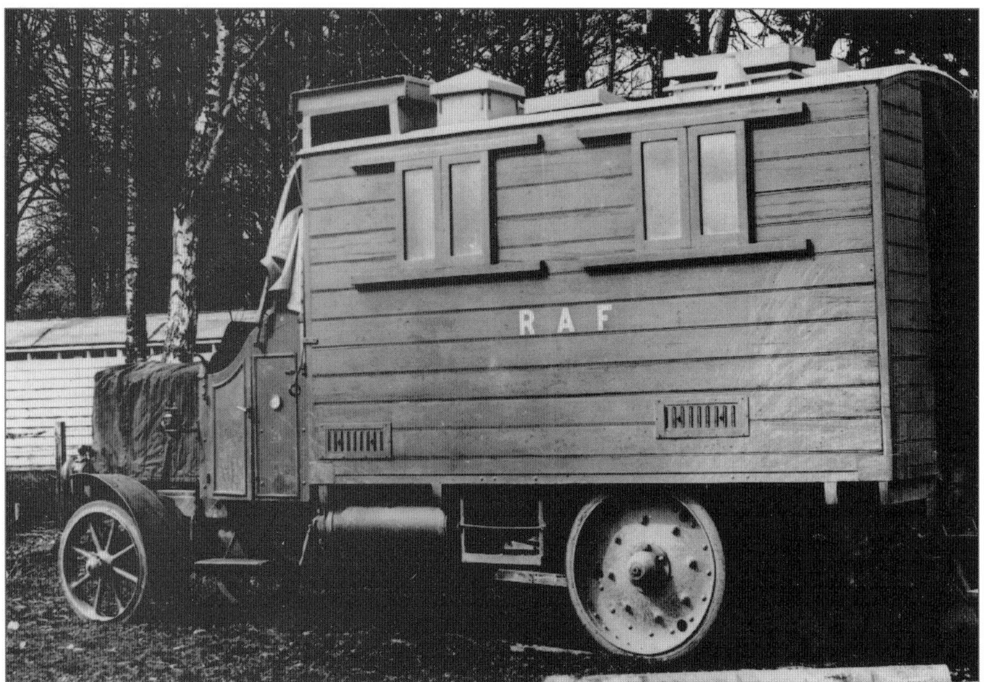


RAF photographic van, 1925. From the early days of activity at Leuchars reconnaissance photography played an important part in airbase work, and this was honed to a high degree of expertise in the Second World War. For instance in 1943 540 Squadron carried out photographic sorties over Berlin and the North German ports.

Valentine's Series view of Guardbridge Paper Mills, *c*. 1900. A medieval hamlet developed in the Guardbridge area as a consequence of use of the river crossings at the River Eden and the Mottray Burn. The village still retains its early fifteenth-century bridge – 'the lie gare brig' – built by Bishop Henry Wardlaw of St Andrews (1404–40); some further construction was carried out by order of Archbishop James Beaton (1522–39). The modern village owes its birth and development to the paper mill. The mill was founded in 1873 on the site of the old Seggie Distillery of *c*. 1810, and construction was completed in August 1874. The quays of Seggie Distillery on the River Eden, incidentally, were the ancient anchorages for the medieval port of St Andrews – known as the 'Water of Eden'. Large schooners and sloops used these anchorages well into Victorian times. The paper mill site was extended in 1882 to the north by purchasing former brewery buildings. By 1888 electric power was installed and the first telephones in 1910; in 1918 the mill's generators were supplying electricity to nearby Leuchars airbase. In 1967 the firm merged to form the Culter Guardbridge paper mill. GB Papers became James River Fine Papers during 1984–95; and in 1995 the firm became Curtis Fine Papers.

This is the earliest known picture of Guardbridge paper mill, which was completed in 1874. The now demolished workmen's cottages, on the right, were erected in 1875. The railway line for the mill linked with the St Andrews–Leuchars Junction Railway (first opened in 1852). The mill site had been extended to the north in 1882.

The extension of the mill site was completed by the 1950s. The first land reclamation scheme was begun in 1897; work began on reclaiming the north bank in 1947. To the top of the picture is seen the Mottray Channel.

Guardbridge No. 1 machine with engineers in the 1930s. The No. 1 machine had been laid down in 1873 and it was to have an output of 30–35 tons of paper a week. A mechanics' workshop was set up in 1876 and a second machine (No. 2) was installed in 1878.

A large number of women were employed at Guardbridge. In the early days of the mill the rag sorters were all women. Female labour was also the bulwark of the paper overhauling and in the packing department.

Esparto grass for papermaking lies in the yard of this view of the papermill at Guardbridge village looking south. A grass store had been built in 1882. The shortages of raw material during the First and Second World Wars led to the mill using local straw; esparto pulp was used from 1972.

The southern development of the mill takes shape. The now vanished rail link is seen to the top right. On 6 January 1969 British Rail closed its St Andrews branch line. To the right, above the tree line, is Seggie House and Estate, bought by the paper mill directors in 1917.

Guardbridge paper mill, looking north and north-west, across the Mottray Burn. The first company houses at Innerbridge were built during 1888, and the village school (mid-left) in 1890. River Terrace was developed from 1913.

Mr and Mrs James Stewart (he became Managing Director of the paper mill in 1923 and was Hon. President of the Club) sit with the trophy winners of the Guardbridge Miniature Rifle Club team, following the award of trophies in 1933. The team members and officials were J.P. Black, R. Coutts, J. Muckersie, W. Mann, A.B. Learmouth, D. Pratt, W. Jack, J. Jack, J. Donaldson and D. Duff.

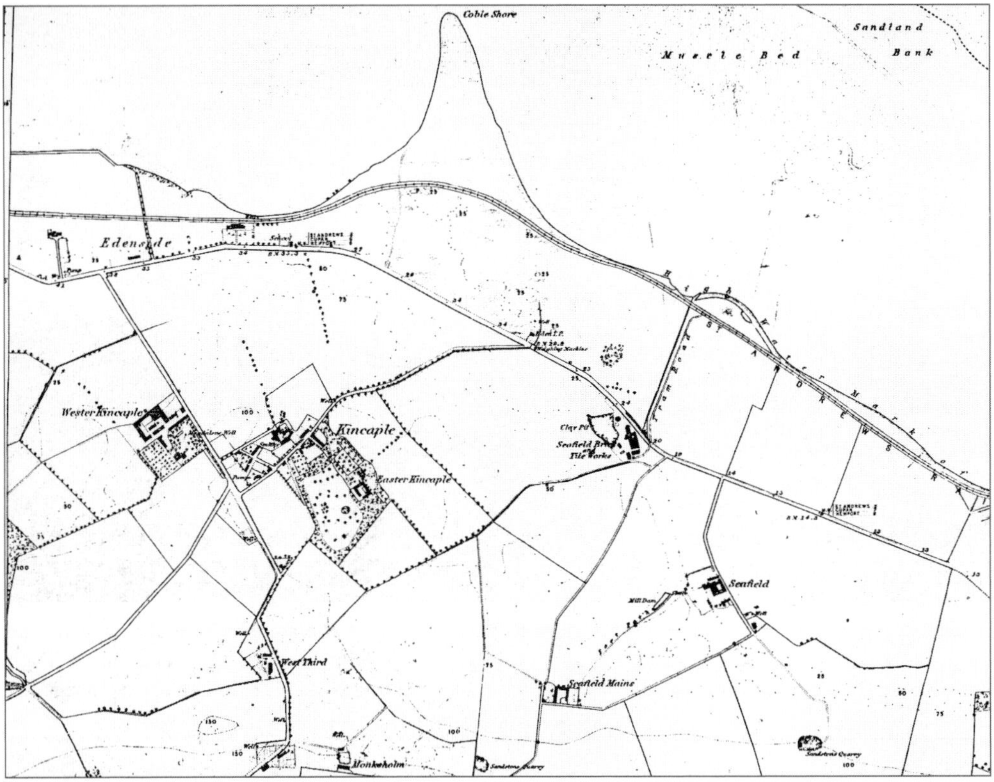

Seafield Clay Pit and Pottery, Brick and Tile Works, founded in about 1850, was last owned by the Wilson family. The map shows the flat-car narrow gauge Tram Road linking the site (across the St Andrews–Guardbridge road) with the main railway line at the work's own siding. The farm marked Seafield is now Easter Kincaple.

Entrance to Seafield works, *c.* 1928. Founded by Alexander Meldrum of Kincaple, it was run by Thomas Wilson & Son from about 1912 to 1942, although the works almost entirely closed in 1940 on the death of Mr Wilson Jr.

To the right stands the now vanished Wilson's cottage, and the four kiln chimneys are clearly seen. The larger chimney rises above the steam engine boiler house. The kilns were fired by coal mainly from Radernie pit, Peat Inn, and Dundee. Stacks of tiles and field drainage pipes are seen in the foreground.

A Seafield worker stands in front of the brick store shed, *c.* 1928. As the products of the works were mainly a seasonal job, many of the workers in the firm's history doubled up as farm labourers. Clay was dug on site.

Thomas Wilson stands at his pottery wheel. Here he made a small range of flower pots, bulb bowls, milk coolers and vases. It appears that he was the only one who could throw the clay and work the wheel.

Some products from the Seafield works. The pottery hen on her basket nest is a money box made by Thomas Wilson for his son. The brick displays the works' name die imprint. The works were demolished in about 1950.

J. Dryburgh's 'platinotype' photograph of George Bruce (1825–1904) at 'Outer Luckie', Boarhills Creek, 1883. A lifeboat worked out of Boarhills from 1865 at the behest of St Andrews benefactor George Bruce. The lifeboatmen – known as 'Bruce's Own' – served here until 1895, latterly aboard the *John and James Mills*. At this site the Swedish brigantine *Napoleon* came to grief in 1864.

George L. Fleming's popular postcard – printed in Saxony – of Lumbo Farm, near St Andrews, *c.* 1900. The lands of Lumbo once formed part of the demesne of the Augustinian Priory of St Andrews.

St Andrews from the southern boundaries, by Nelson Street and Largo Road and Claybraes farm, 1925.

The LNER railway line leads the eye to the western development of St Andrews at Pilmour Links, Gibson Place and Windmill Road, 1925.

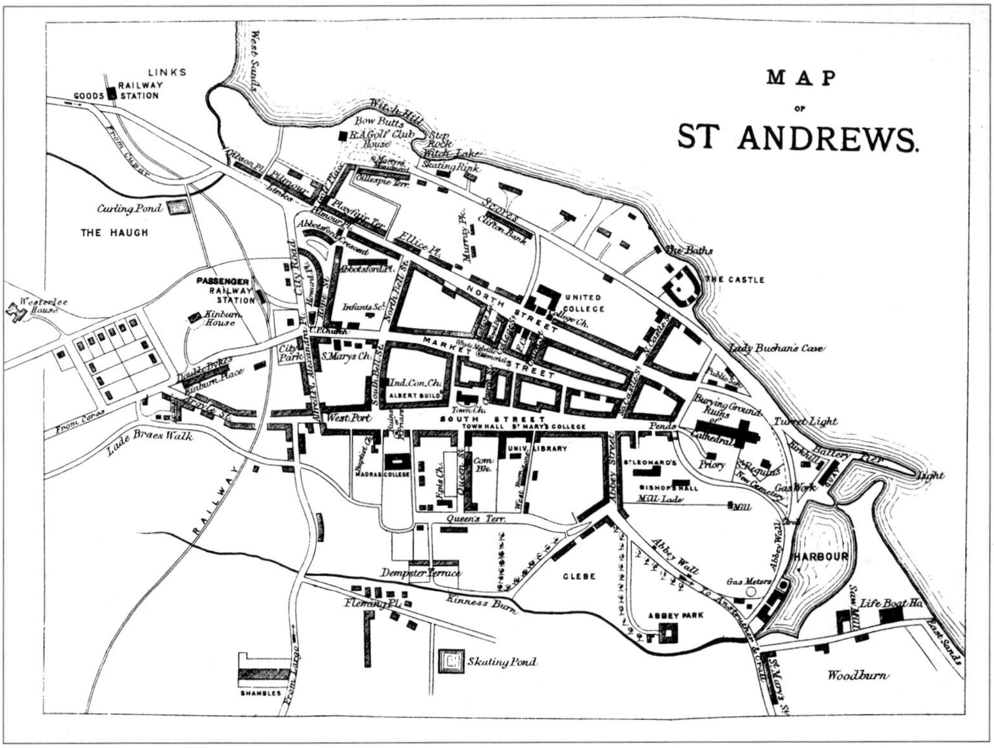

St Andrews street plan, 1887.

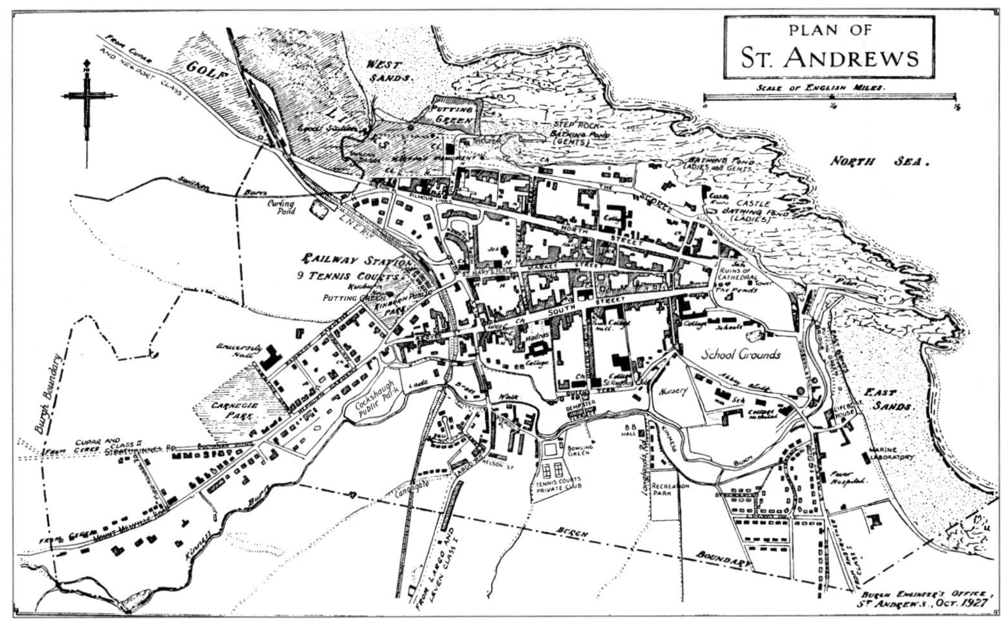


St Andrews burgh boundaries, 1927.

# ACKNOWLEDGEMENTS

Most of the photographs in this book come from the collection held by the St Andrews Preservation Trust. They represent the work of many St Andrews photographers known and unknown. They are supplemented by some other sources and the author wishes to thank the following for making these images available for inclusion: St Andrews Research and Lecture Projects, NE Fife District Council, St Andrews Curling Club, John Harrison, Forte Plc, RAF Leuchars, the Baron and Baroness of Earlshall, and Curtis Fine Papers, Guardbridge.

The picture of the Byre Theatre on page 75 was gifted to the author by the late Alex Paterson MBE.

A number of special thanks are due to the following for their assistance in the compiling of this volume: Emily Cook, Curator of the St Andrews Preservation Trust Museum, Mr Gordon Christie, Flt Lt J.E. Taylor, and Mr Alan Milne.